GILBERT AND SULLIVAN

and their world

LESLIE BAILY

GILBERT AND SULLIVAN

and their world

THAMES AND HUDSON
LONDON

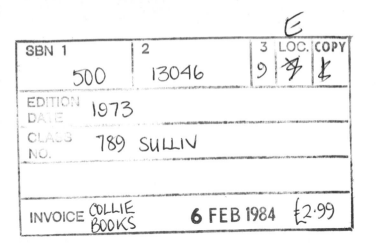
AUTHOR'S NOTE

Since I wrote *The Gilbert and Sullivan Book* twenty years ago, further research has uncovered fresh facts, while others have been revised. The present volume concentrates on the span of Gilbert and Sullivan's lives alone, and the opportunity has been taken to reassess the cultural contribution they made, with D'Oyly Carte, to their world, to posterity and not least to the gaiety of nations.

© *1973 Thames and Hudson Ltd, London*

Reprinted 1973

Printed in Great Britain by Jarrold and Sons Ltd, Norwich

ISBN 0 500 13046 9

THE KING OF VICTORIAN JESTERS was born seven months before a teenage Victoria succeeded to the throne. Of all the products and modes of that solid reign, seemingly so permanent and rigidly right-side-up to the good Queen and her people, one of the few which remain alive today is the topsy-turvy art known as Gilbert and Sullivan Opera. Such an eccentric destiny is proper to our subject, or to one half of it: Sir William Schwenck Gilbert, whose terse reply to the *Strand Magazine*'s enquiry as to his origin was: 'Date of birth, 18 November 1836. Birthplace, 17 Southampton Street, Strand, in the house of my grandfather, who had known Dr Johnson, Garrick and Reynolds, and who was the last man in London, I believe, who wore Hessian boots and a pig-tail.'

The Gilberts had originally been a sturdy family of yeomen in the south of England. W.S.G.'s heyday passion for yachting gave an outlet for a sneaking belief that he was related to Sir Humphrey Gilbert, a whim evidenced when he built a fine mansion in Kensington and had a stone model of Sir Humphrey's ship mounted on the gable. A guileless visitor who asked whether it was H.M.S. *Pinafore* was answered: 'Sir, I don't put my trade-mark on my house.' There was in fact no relationship with the Elizabethan mariner, but at any rate W.S.G.'s father was a naval surgeon; he married a Scot, Anne

The entrance to the Strand in 1841, then the centre of a pleasant residential district in which W. S. Gilbert had been born in 1836. Gilbert's connections with the area persisted: part of his education took place at King's College in the Strand, and three theatres in which his operas were performed were built nearby – the Gaiety, the Opéra Comique and the Savoy.

5

The abduction of 'Bab' recollected in adulthood. Gilbert used his child-hood nickname as a pseudonym when, years later, he began to produce the comic verses and draw-ings with which he first attracted the attention of the Victorian public. (*Right*) William Gilbert senior. His relations with his wife Anne were often strained, but the naval surgeon remained close to his son all his life and took great pride in W.S.G.'s later success.

Morris, and they lived in genteel Hammersmith, where Gilbert Senior attempted a literary career in his retirement. It was conspicuously unsuccessful, perhaps because, as he wrote: 'From my earliest childhood the ridiculous has thrust itself into every action of my life. I have been haunted through my whole existence by the absurd.' His son inherited this idiosyncrasy but put it to more profitable use. At two years of age he was stolen by a couple of ingratiating brigands in Naples while being pushed out by Nurse; fifty years later Gilbert the Savoyard (who never wasted anything) plotted for a princely babe to be stolen and lodged, 'gaily prattling, with a highly respectable gondolier' in that high-spirited fantasy *The Gondoliers*.

In real life an irate naval surgeon recovered Baby Schwenck for a £25 ransom, a bargain for posterity. W.S.G., born with a sharp tongue in his mouth into a comfortable home, was duly dispatched to Great Ealing School where he sharpened it further. He was a boy of keen intellect and a tendency to domineer; he had a gift for art (not conducive to renown in a Victorian grammar school), and, at fifteen, he nursed a passion deprecated by most upper-middle-class parents: fired by playing Guy Fawkes in a school melodrama, he went to see Charles Keen in *The Corsican Brothers* and forthwith presented himself boldly at the stage door to ask for a job. Keen sent him packing, back to his books at Ealing. Gilbert's adolescent experiences of finding his feet were chillingly abortive, as we shall see.

Meanwhile a clarinettist named Thomas Sullivan was playing in the orchestra at another London theatre, the Royal Surrey. He earned a guinea a week there, and walked home to a tiny working-class house on the un-fashionable side of the Thames, in Bolwell Terrace, a turning off the Lambeth Walk. Outwardly it was a mean and ugly house (it has lately been swept away by slum clearance); inside, it was a joyous cradle of music, for Tom loved every form of the art. In the front parlour was a piano where he gave lessons. In the bedroom above Arthur Seymour Sullivan was born, with a silver trumpet in his mouth, on 13 May 1842. There was nothing abortive or even tentative about his early steps. 'When I was not more than four or five years old it became perfectly evident that my career in life must be music and nothing else,' he declared later. 'When I was barely five I used to go to the piano and make discoveries for myself.' He was a likeable boy, a rare charmer. He was to charm the ears of a great public and it was marvellous how the Lambeth boy became transfigured into the polished Doctor of Music, knight of the realm, boon companion of princes of the arts and royalty, and lifelong bachelor whose secret intimacies were cherished by the most sophisticated of women.

From a mixture of Irish, Italian and possibly Jewish blood Arthur Sullivan drew his prodigious musicality, his gay love of life, and the sentimentality which occasionally overlaid his sterling sentiments. His mother, Maria Clementina Coghlan, came of an artistic Italian family. His grandfather Sullivan from County Cork became a sergeant in the British Army, guarding the exiled Napoleon on St Helena. He ended his life as a Chelsea Pensioner four years before Arthur was born.

In the heart of Cockney London, genial Maria and Tom Sullivan dreamed and schemed for their sons, Frederic and Arthur. Amid poverty they main-tained respectability. Maria went out to teach at a Catholic school. Then Tom lifted the family to a superior environment by becoming bandmaster at the Royal Military College, Sandhurst. 'He is what we have lacked – a real musician,' pronounced his Colonel.

The Sullivans moved to 171 Yorktown Road in Camberley: 'I remember going to London by horse-coach from Yorktown to see the Great Exhibition of 1851. There was no railway near us,' recalled Arthur later. That year when he first walked the iron-pillared aisles of the Crystal Palace in Hyde Park was also the year when the schoolboy from Ealing was spurned at Keen's stage door.

In 1851 the only reputable musical entertainments in the theatres of London were foreign operas like Donizetti's *L'Elisir d'Amore* and Meyerbeer's *Robert the Devil*; and the Queen went to see *The Magic Flute* at Covent Garden (then called the 'Royal Italian Opera'). There was no English musical theatre. The nearest approach to it was *The Far West, or the Emigrant's Progress from the Old World to the New*, by Henry Russell, depicting life in

Sullivan's birthplace at 8 Bolwell Terrace, Lambeth. In this mean side street the boy who was to become the friend of princes spent the first three years of his life amid impoverished respectability.

the Canadian wilds and tricked out with Russell's tuneful songs, among them 'Cheer, Boys, Cheer' and 'A Life on the Ocean Wave'. There was plenty of bucolic song in pubs and midnight supper rooms such as the Coal Hole in the Strand. There were even American musical shows in London: Hector Berlioz, who came from France to see the Great Exhibition, wrote of how fascinated he was to hear in London 'nigger minstrel troupes' from the USA singing the ballads of Stephen Foster, who published 'The Old Folks at Home' in 1851.

Thus, apart from the lusty songs of pubs or music-halls, the British had little of contemporary native music to put into the international shop window during the Great Exhibition of the Industry of All Nations; when Sullivan

The Crystal Palace shortly after its erection in Hyde Park in 1851. Sullivan was to be associated with the building for most of his life, and several of his serious works received their first performance under its roof.

went to the Crystal Palace the music he was most likely to hear on its several mighty organs was that of Handel's *Messiah*.

It was appropriately romantic in the Sullivan mode that the Crystal Palace should be among his earliest memories, for some of the greatest moments of his future life, and some of his closest friends, were intimately connected with it. One of the engineers who built it, John Scott Russell, was the father of Rachel, a girl whom later Sullivan nearly married. Sullivan was haunted by the romantic, as Gilbert was haunted by the ridiculous. And both were inspired by both to mix a cordial, now sweet, now dry, which English-speaking people the world over liked very well – eventually. A taste for it had first to be created.

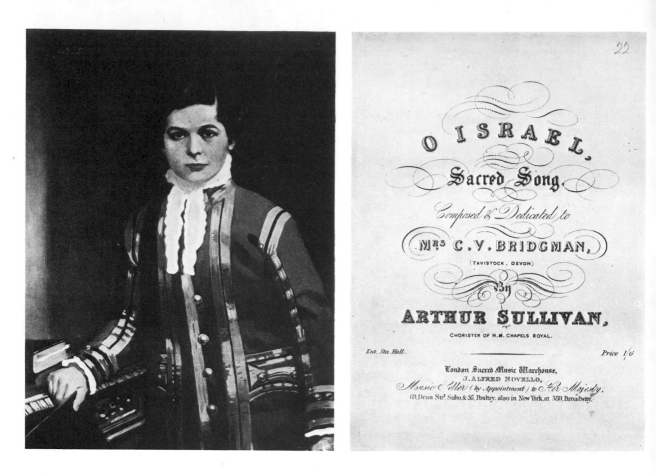

Sullivan as a chorister of the Chapel Royal. His admission into this exclusive clan represented the first fulfilment of his ambitions: 'it means everything to me', he wrote. His fellow choristers included Alfred Cellier (composer of *Dorothy*) and his brother François, both of whom later conducted Gilbert and Sullivan operas. (*Right*) The title-page of 'O Israel', Sullivan's first published music.

From Sandhurst Tom Sullivan progressed to a professorship at the Military School of Music, Kneller Hall. Both jobs were important to his son's formative years. Tom took him to band practices where the boy picked up a working knowledge of every instrument. So stirred the spirit that was to inspire marches fit to raise the dead, be it 'Onward Christian Soldiers' or those in *Iolanthe*; but in Sullivan's adolescence, when he became a boarder at an academy for young gentlemen in Paddington, his first efforts at composition were of the order of a sacred song, 'O Israel'. The religiosity of the day appealed strongly to this sensitive boy and this early choice foreshadows the dichotomy within Sullivan between the devout and the frivolous, between oratorio and comic opera.

Lucky Sullivan! His enchanting treble and his prodigious knowledge of music caught the attention of the most influential musician in the land, Sir George Smart. He brought pressure to bear on the Reverend Thomas Helmore, Master of Her Majesty's Chapel Royal at St James's Palace, with the result that Arthur was admitted to the élite choir of boys who sang in royal palaces and on great national occasions, wearing scarlet and gold uniforms. Under Helmore's stern rule they had their own boarding-school at 6 Cheyne Walk. Sullivan wrote home: 'M was caned today because he did not know the meaning of fortissimo.'

In 1854 the Crystal Palace, having been removed to Sydenham, was reopened as a concert hall with ear-shattering effect by a mammoth chorus, an orchestra of two hundred and fifty, and the bands of the Grenadier and Coldstream Guards, in the presence of the Queen and the Prince Consort – seventeen hundred performers in all, among whom sang Arthur Sullivan and the choristers of the Chapel Royal. Musically it was an atrocious performance. Arthur Sullivan must have rated much higher two events in the following year. 'O Israel' was sold in the shops, his first publication; and Sir George Smart himself conducted at the Chapel Royal an anthem entitled 'Sing Unto the Lord', by Sullivan. The Bishop of London was present, and Arthur proudly reported to his parents that 'he called me up to him in the vestry and said it was very clever, and said that perhaps I should be writing an oratorio some day. But he said there was Something Higher.

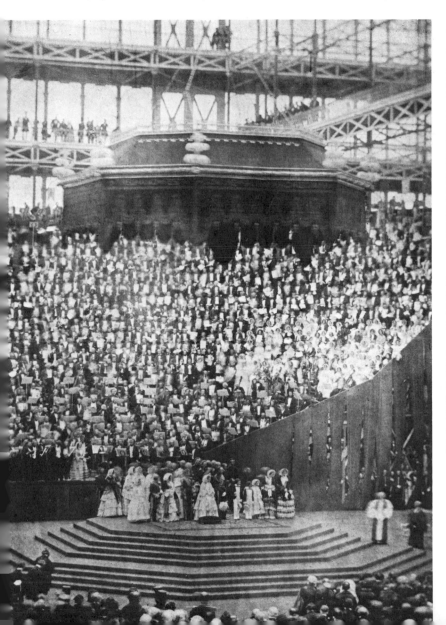

Maria Sullivan, the composer's mother. An abiding influence on her son, her death in 1882 was a severe blow.

(*Left*) The reopening of the Crystal Palace after its move to Sydenham, 10 June 1854. The young Arthur Sullivan was among the seventeen hundred performers, writing home 'I cannot tell you by letter of the grandeur of the scene'.

King's College, London, where Gilbert studied in the General Literature and Science Department from 1853 to 1857.

to attend to, and then Mr Helmore said that I was a very good boy indeed. Whereupon he shook hands with me, with half a sovereign.' This was the first fee he ever received for the performance of one of his own works. Very soon he was 'first boy' at the Chapel Royal.

Gilbert had passed out of Ealing School as an unspectacular head boy and entered King's College, London, preparatory to some safe and respectable vocation suited to his social class, but one small incident when he was a schoolboy was predictive. He had caught typhoid fever, the nineteenth-century scourge often arising from bad drains. Emaciated and with shaven head, he recuperated in France, where one day in the street he watched Napoleon III and the Empress Eugénie pass in procession. In an exercise book he wrote:

> When the horses, white with foam,
> Drew the Empress to her home
> From the place whence she did roam,
> The Empress she did see
> The Gilbert Familee.
> To the Emperor she said:
> 'How beautiful the head
> Of that youth of gallant mien,
> Cropped so neat and close and clean –
> Though I own he's rather lean.'
> Said the Emperor: 'It is!
> And I never saw a phiz more wonderful than 'is.'

This adolescent verse was to Gilbert what 'O Israel' was to Sullivan. If these two were so different in early creativity, in upbringing and character, where was the common chord? Both had a strong sense of humour based on everyday life. Sullivan of Lambeth began with his feet firmly on the ground; he was never ashamed of tuning his music to the hearts of the people, straightforwardly, whether in fun or in sentiment. Gilbert's wit had an astringency partly inherited from the naval surgeon and partly acquired in the hard years of finding his feet. He looked at life through his legs, upside down, which can be both refreshing and amusing.

Sullivan, typically, was the first to get his name into public print (the *Illustrated London News*, 1855) when he sang at the Hanover Square Rooms, London's centre for serious music. Here had performed J. C. Bach, Haydn, Liszt, Mendelssohn, Joachim, and this year Wagner made his first public appearance in England there, conducting the Philharmonic Society's symphony concerts, and thundering at the mediocrity of performance. English orchestral playing was extremely bad at this period. Indeed, music in general was at a low ebb.

Gilbert, after turning King's College Scientific Society into a Dramatic Society, pocketed a modest B A. His determination to win the Crimean War had been frustrated by the arrival of peace. He was rising twenty-one when Sullivan, aged fourteen, won the Mendelssohn Scholarship at the Royal Academy of Music, the youngest among seventeen competitors, and the first winner of this coveted prize. Gilbert got a job as clerk in the Civil Service at £120 a year, 'one of the worst bargains any government ever made,' he said. He hated it.

The Hanover Square Concert Rooms, until their closure in 1874 the scene of many of the most significant musical events in Victorian London.

Sketches by 'Bab': Gilbert sought escape from his depressing clerical job by joining the 5th West Yorkshire Militia, later becoming a captain in the Royal Aberdeenshire Militia. The meticulous attention he devoted to the uniforms worn in his comic operas is evidence of his life-long interest in military affairs.

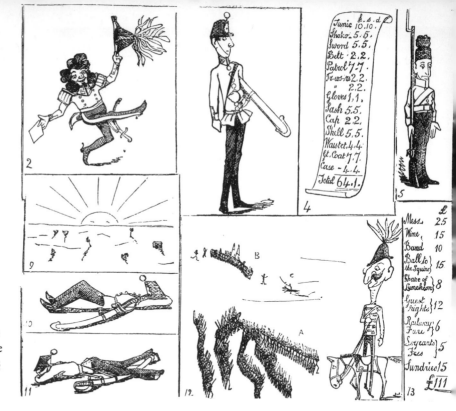

At the Academy Sullivan delighted his professors and loved every minute, yet he never appeared a prig in the eyes of his fellow students, for he had both tact and high spirits: 'Dearest Mother and Father, – Every time I have made up my mind to sit down and write to you some fellow or other is sure to turn me away from it by asking me to come and lead our band, which, by the by, consists of two French "squeakers" which produce a twangy sound like an oboe, two combs, a cover of a book for a drum. By the bye, I have sold 22s. worth of songs to different gentlemen.' Perched on his office stool meanwhile, Gilbert often had a jingle in his mind as he scratched at a blot; he now ventured to post one of these verses, called 'Satisfied Isaiah Jones', to Fleet Street. It came back, but with a helpful hint: 'The Editor of *Once a Week* regrets that he cannot use the enclosed clever and amusing poem owing to its length.'

Gilbert's first appearance in print was when a lady with the glorious name of Euphrosyne Parepa-Rosa sang at the Promenade Concerts an aria from *Manon Lescaut*, and 'I went to those concerts to enjoy the intense gratification of standing at the elbow of any promenader who might be reading my translation, and wondering to myself what that promenader would say if he knew that the gifted creature who had written the very words he was reading was at that moment standing within a yard of him?' But Gilbert had to endure four years in the Civil Service, relieved only by zestful exercises carried out as a volunteer in the 5th West Yorkshire Militia; then he came into a legacy of £300. Straightaway he sent in his resignation, on 'the happiest day of my life. With £100 I paid my call to the bar (I had previously entered myself as a student at the Middle Temple), with another £100 I obtained access to a conveyancer's chambers, and with the third £100 I furnished a set of chambers of my own, and began life afresh as a barrister-at-law.'

The ridiculous still haunted him, even in court. One day when an old woman was accused of picking pockets Gilbert made an impassioned speech for her defence; but she was sentenced to eighteen months' hard labour, whereupon she hurled a heavy boot at him. Gilbert was not slow to use the incident in a short story in the *Cornhill Magazine*. He was making slow ground as a writer, and in four years at the Bar he did badly. In a threadbare Pimlico boarding-house he had written by the age of twenty-four some fifteen farces and burlesques; not one was accepted.

Also in Pimlico but unknown to Gilbert, Arthur Sullivan and his architect brother Fred were members of an amateur dramatic society. Arthur brought along twenty-six music students as an orchestra, which he conducted. It was his first experience in front of a curtain. At the Academy his promise was such that in 1858 an extension of his Mendelssohn Scholarship sent him to the Conservatory at Leipzig, the finest school of music in Europe.

To Sullivan his visit to Germany was more than an education. It was a pilgrimage. He was always highly sensitive to atmosphere; now he sensed near him the great composers of the past. 'I took lessons in counterpoint in the very room where Bach wrote all his works when in Leipzig, so you can imagine the atmosphere of that room as being impregnated with counterpoint and fugue.' One of his tutors, the virtuoso pianist Moscheles, had heard Beethoven play. Sullivan's first ambition was to be a pianist, but during three years at Leipzig he developed excitingly as composer and conductor:

Leipzig in the mid-nineteenth century. The musical capital of Europe, its Conservatory had been founded by Mendelssohn in 1843.

Rosamund Barnett, Sullivan's fellow student at Leipzig to whom he dedicated an early love-song. She later married the celebrated novelist R.E. Francillon. (*Right*) Arthur Sullivan as a student at the Leipzig Conservatory: 'in England there was very little more for me to learn.'

'It was such fun standing up there and conducting that large orchestra! I can fancy Mother saying "Bless his little heart! How it must have beaten."' He met great figures of the day – Liszt, Spohr, Schumann – and at least one of the next generation, his fellow student Grieg. He was 'received' everywhere, and made his entry into German society graciously: 'It was Sullivan's very nature to ingratiate himself with everyone that crossed his path. He always wanted to make an impression, and what is more always succeeded in doing so. He was a natural courtier.' So he was summed up by a student from England, Clara Barnett, whose sister Rosamund was perhaps Sullivan's first love. He was a regular devil with the girls, remarked Clara.

Sullivan's music for *The Tempest*, his first major work, was heard at one of the famous Gewandhaus concerts at Leipzig in his last year as a student. At nineteen he returned to England, determined to make people sit up, not only by his own music but by his advanced ideas: he was an enthusiast for the neglected Schubert and, more surprisingly, for Schumann, whose music was unattractively modernistic to most. Sullivan's *Tempest* was privately performed in London and George Grove recognized its importance; as Secretary of the Crystal Palace he proposed a public performance there. Sullivan wrote to Clara Rogers: 'My *Tempest* music is progressing and going to take the world by "storm".'

There may seem to be no connection whatsoever between the return of this amiable but pushing young composer and the offering posted by an impoverished barrister in the same year to the journal *Fun*, edited by H. J. Byron. But the stars are on their converging courses. Byron spotted the value of the Gilbertian quality for *Fun* (nicknamed 'the penny *Punch*'), and Victorian drawing-rooms were thereafter assaulted by a cascade of comic and often pungent verses with zany illustrations, anonymous at first, then printed over Gilbert's childhood pet name of 'Bab'. Meanwhile the first public performance of *The Tempest* at the Crystal Palace, on 5 April 1862, caused a furore; it sounded the Sullivan keynote of gaiety and romance. 'It is no exaggeration to say that I woke up the next morning and found myself famous. All musical London went down to the Crystal Palace to hear the second performance. Charles Dickens met me there. He seized my hand in his iron grip and said, "I don't pretend to know much about music, but I do know I've been listening to a very great work."' *The Times* approved, the *Manchester Guardian* called it 'masterly', and a wide public applauded its somewhat Mendelssohnian idiom (a sure bet) touched with Sullivan's specific sense of fun.

The first issue of *Fun*, 1862. The editor's early request to Gilbert to contribute to it 'every week for the term of my natural life', as Gilbert put it, was to result in the *Bab Ballads*.

Gilbert's *Bab Ballads*, as he called them when they were published as a book, were a major contribution of English fun, with an unmatched element of nonsense:

> *Strike the concertina's melancholy string!*
> *Blow the spirit-stirring harp like anything!*
> *Let the piano's martial blast*
> *Rouse the echoes of the past,*
> *For of Agib, Prince of Tartary I sing!*
> *Of Agib, who, amid Tartaric scenes*
> *Wrote a lot of ballet-music in his teens:*
> *His gentle spirit rolls*
> *In the melody of souls —*
> *Which is pretty, but I don't know what it means!*

The *Bab Ballads* are the Savoy Operas in embryo, especially *Iolanthe*, *H.M.S. Pinafore* and *Patience*. But an embryo can be ugly: a few of Gilbert's notions and some of his original caricatures in the *Ballads* were savage. Victorians in the 1860s laughed – a little uneasily. They were never quite sure whether Bab was being serious underneath his nonsense. In one of the ballads he wrote of dwelling 'in topsyturveydom ... where right is wrong and wrong is right; where white is black, and black is white.' In real life his satire was often based on such inversions.

The world of Arthur Sullivan was a harmonious one where the white notes were definitely white and the black notes were always black. *The Tempest* shot him into Society, but he still needed to earn a living; so he took pupils at his lodgings in Pimlico, taught at the Chapel Royal, and became organist at the fashionable (of course) Church of St Michael, Chester Square. Being short of tenors and basses he recruited a dozen bobbies from the nearby police station (again 'of course', for here is Sullivan's lowly pedigree impelling him to break class barriers).

Holidaying in Paris with Dickens and Grove, he met old Rossini. The composer of *The Barber of Seville*, now seventy years old, white-haired and rheumatic, sat at the piano with the young man while they improvised duets from *The Tempest*. 'I think that Rossini first inspired me with a love for the stage and things operatic, and this led to my undertaking the duties of organist at the Royal Italian Opera (London),' said Sullivan. There, at Covent Garden, in the ballet *L'Ile Enchantée*, Sullivan's music was first heard in a theatre. Often he was called upon to run up 'a few bars of tiddle-iddle-um' as he called it to suit last-minute changes in the programme; it was an invaluable apprenticeship.

Gilbert entered the theatre by another door when the dramatist T. W. Robertson (of *Caste*) invited him to watch rehearsals, a useful lesson to any budding author. Robertson also recommended him to St James's Theatre, where a Christmas play was urgently needed in 1866. There a parody on Donizetti's opera *L'Elisir d'Amore* called *Dulcamara: or, The Little Duck and the Great Quack* earned Gilbert a meagre £30. Such parodies, or burlesques as Victorians called them, were the best the London theatre could do in light entertainment. They did *not* use original music.

Gioacchino Rossini (1792–1868), who inspired Sullivan with a love of 'things operatic'.

Sullivan was also selling cheap in the 1860s: 'I was ready to undertake everything that came my way.' He set Shakespearean lyrics at five guineas apiece; popular ballads he sold outright at ten guineas. They became the rage of the middle and upper classes. When the Scandinavian Princess Alexandra came to Britain he hailed her with 'Bride from the North', and when she married the Prince of Wales (later King Edward VII) Sullivan's *Wedding March* was played through the length of the land. There was no radio to flash a reputation to the ends of the earth overnight, but Sullivan's songs were lavishly displayed in the music shops, and he was in demand as a conductor of orchestral and choral concerts. During his studentship in Germany he had 'got savage . . . at the sneering way in which they talk of "England's art"'; now he felt a call to remove that stigma, and the power within him to do so. Since the Elizabethans – Byrd, Tallis, Orlando Gibbons – three giants of music had lived in England. Purcell had died in 1695, Handel in 1759, Mendelssohn in 1847; the last two were German born. There had been English composers in a lighter vein, such as Thomas Arne with his ballad opera *Love in a Village* (1762) and John Gay of *The Beggar's Opera* (1728), both more than a century before Sullivan entered the field. For the present, he thought of 'England's art' in terms of the concert platform – of symphony and oratorio. His duty was to spread good music throughout Britain.

So in the 1860s and the 1870s this genial missionary travelled to the industrial cities of the Midlands and the North, where musical festivals were

The Italian Opera House (now the Royal Opera House), Covent Garden, where Sullivan was organist for a time and learnt valuable lessons in the art of tailoring music for the stage.

Detail of William Frith's painting of the wedding of the future King Edward VII and Princess Alexandra of Denmark on 10 March 1863. Sullivan composed his highly popular *Wedding March* for the occasion.

set amid the 'dark satanic mills', and the people gathered to sing at their festivals under the guttering gas-lamps of town halls. At Birmingham, Manchester, Norwich, Glasgow, and later especially at Leeds, Arthur Sullivan became the musical idol of these people, their conductor, their Leader who carried the key to the Promised Land where music should transcend all the ugliness of their daily lives. There was no one else in the field who combined the musicianship and the magnetic personality for such a role, though others contributed to the upsurge of choralism, notably Hullah, Costa, Hallé, Benedict, and especially Joseph Barnby, who had been Sullivan's runner-up in the competition for the Mendelssohn Scholarship in 1856.

Sullivan was resting in Ireland when one wet night while driving in a jaunting-car near Belfast 'the whole first movement of a symphony came into my head'. On 10 March 1866 he stood under the vast glass roof of the Crystal Palace conducting his symphony, called *In Ireland*, an audience of three thousand at his back, including his professor of composition of Royal Academy days, Sir John Goss. It was Sullivan's greatest opportunity yet, and his greatest success. Goss wrote: 'You may prove a worthy peer of the great symphonists,' though a grand panjandrum on *The Times* lectured Sullivan to 'abjure Mendelssohn, even Beethoven, and above all Schumann', and to look to the 'legitimate models' of Haydn and Mozart. But the three thousand acclaimed and Sullivan bobbed on and off the platform like the born showman that he was. Gilbert was not that type of showman. He once remarked that he would as soon invite friends to supper after a first night as after an amputation at the hip-joint.

A powerful influence in Sullivan's life for several years was Rachel, the bluestocking daughter of that important man of affairs, John Scott Russell, FRS. Tirelessly she spurred Sullivan on to higher things, in hundreds of love-letters: 'Is the Symph in D getting on? Do write it, my bird. It is the language in which you talk to me. I also want you to write an octet. Mendelssohn's is splendid, and I am sure you could do a glorious thing. Will you?' Sullivan never wrote a second symphony, nor married Rachel. Gilbert, however, at thirty-one, took as wife seventeen-year-old Lucy Agnes Turner, the daughter of an officer in the Indian Army. She was a dainty creature, small, fair-haired and blue-eyed; W.S.G. called her 'Kitten'. They settled in

A sketch of his wife from Gilbert's notebooks.

W. S. Gilbert and 'Kitten' shortly after their marriage in 1867.

Kensington, and she never spurred him on to anything. He did not need it. Crossing to France on their honeymoon, he wrote a Bab Ballad. Fortunately, Kitten had a sense of humour.

Gilbert's few diaries were terse, recording little more than everyday affairs. Sullivan's twenty diaries were such a depository of his *affaires* and professional emotions that he invented his own shorthand code and sealed them with brass locks. But Gilbert's doodle-creatures, sketched in the margins of his plot-books and manuscripts, give some guide to the man. They fall into two distinct categories. There are the *Bab Ballad* grotesques, satirical and even savagely satirical. And then, almost as though by another artist, there are the dainty girls and fairies he drew in his notebooks and used, occasionally, for book illustrations. Behind the satirist, the sentimentalist. Even in the most savage of *Bab Ballad* sketches, if a young woman is introduced she is inevitably bewitching (elderly women are another thing); likewise in the comic operas.

It has been said that this tall and lusty man, spending so much of his theatre life in the company of pretty women, *must* have had *affaires*. But not a shred of real evidence has appeared. We must not blur Gilbert's world with modern permissive preconceptions. One evening he drove to his house with a lady; both intended to go on to the theatre, but Gilbert found his wife out, so the lady had to sit in the carriage while he changed indoors. This punctiliousness was Gilbert's Victorian world; the low necklines and dainty ankles of his notebook nymphs are evidence of the man of sensibility.

After the *Quack* came more burlesques and pantomimes in the most popular vein but of little lasting value. It may seem strange that the innovator of the *Bab Ballads* should open his stage career with commonplace tripe, but the explanation is simple: the *Ballads* had an instant *Punch*-made public among the intelligentsia, ripe for a step into Gilbertian surrealism, whereas in the theatre Gilbert knew as a man of sense as well as nonsense that to make money he had to begin by pleasing – and educating – a wider public. He was also learning a more intricate craft than simple versification. Very soon he was teaching his masters a lesson.

He was angered to find that writers were treated roughly by the almighty producers. His careful plot for *Harlequin Cock-Robin and Jenny Wren*, the Lyceum pantomime of 1867–68, was interrupted for the Fairy Aquarium (with Espinosa's Grand Ballet), and St James's Park After a Snowstorm, not to mention the Electric Light and Magic Fountain patented by M. Delaporte of Paris. In the next issue of *Fun* Gilbert let himself go. He printed the plot of *Harlequin Wilkinson, or the Fairy Pewopener and the Vicar of Pendleton-cum-Turnuptop*, in which at the very height of the drama, when 'the lovers are embracing more than ever', a dozen scenes are interpolated 'to allow time to set a Magic Drinking Fountain, or an Ethereal Wash-hand Basin, or a Chromatic Pump, or a Lime-lit Tub, or any other elaborate property which the Management may think fit to introduce into the story at the last moment.'

Doodles from Gilbert's sketchbooks. The consistent contrast between Gilbert's attitude to young women and his portrayal of the more elderly has in later years given rise to a controversy over his 'cruelty' and 'sadism' which W.S.G. himself would no doubt have found incomprehensible.

Programme fan sold to the audience during the run of Gilbert's *Robert le Diable* at the Gaiety, 1868.

This was the natal cry of Gilbert the stage disciplinarian. Later he was to settle author-producer dissidence characteristically, by doing both jobs himself; but first he had to establish himself as a man of promise in the theatre. The first important recognition of W.S.G.'s gifts was at Christmas 1868 when John Hollingshead opened his Gaiety Theatre with *Robert le Diable, or The Nun, the Dun, and the Son of a Gun*. Gilbert's pun-ridden parody of Meyerbeer's opera *Robert the Devil* was no great guns in itself, but thus began the famous Gaiety burlesque tradition which we shall find playing a curious part in the Gilbert and Sullivan story later.

Gilbert of the burlesque and Sullivan of the symphony worked in worlds a thousand artistic miles apart at this point in their careers. In private life, too, the difference was marked. Whimsical Gilbert nicknamed his wife 'Kitten' or 'Mrs', while the emotional Rachel Scott Russell, after Sullivan had dedicated to her his love-song 'O, Fair Dove! O, Fond Dove!', signed her letters to the composer 'Fond Dove'.

In 1866 an emotional crisis came from another direction to wring music of a different kind from the depths of Arthur Sullivan's despair. Commissioned to compose an orchestral work for the Norwich Festival of 1866, he had become dejected at a total failure of inspiration, with less than a month to go.

Sullivan's song 'O, Fair Dove! O, Fond Dove!' became a best-seller. (*Below*) Part of a letter from Rachel to Sullivan in which she copied out the lyric.

Part of Grove's letter of condolence with, on the back, Sullivan's first sketch for the overture *In Memoriam*, one of the few examples of his serious music which are still played today.

Then came the sudden death of his father Tom. George Grove wrote to Sullivan: 'It's little I can say to comfort you. . . . It was a great thing to him to have lived to see your triumph . . . before your symphony was done it would have been quite a different thing for him.' On Grove's letter Arthur sketched the opening bars of his overture *In Memoriam*, and it was ready for the Festival.

It was Grove who had introduced Arthur Sullivan into the affluent Scott Russell house at Norwood, close to the Crystal Palace. Arthur often dined there, played the piano at parties, with Patti singing, and walked in the hushed and scented garden with Rachel. His memoirs tell us that the dinner guests included writers, artists and musicians. 'We would discuss music, painting, poetry, literature, *and even science* until the clock told us that the last train back to London was nearly due.'

(*Right*) A house-party on the croquet-lawn of the Scott Russells' home at Norwood. Sullivan is on the extreme left, next to John Scott Russell, while Grove sits third from right.

'Even' Scott Russell's science. The condescending afterthought is not surprising: Rachel's father and Sullivan did not get on well. Scott Russell, as an eminent engineer associated with such wonders as Brunel's *Great Eastern*, expected to launch his daughters on copper-bottomed matrimonial matches. He might be Secretary of the Society of Arts but he was more interested in Sullivan's bank balance than his music, a Victorian attitude that infuriated the young man.

'If you are ready to marry me next year then well and good,' wrote Rachel. 'I will tell Mama and Papa when you see the project clear before you without a doubt – free of debt – and then there will be no reasonable objection.' Rachel was a passionate girl, with a cultivated knowledge of music and literature, and a temperament as erratic as Sullivan's. One day she urges him to write an Arthurian grand opera, *Guinevere*, based on Tennyson ('Work at it intensely and religiously, as the old masters worked – like dear old Bach – and it must be a great work'); and next she scolds him for being 'seen in Bond Street in a hansom with Lady Katherine'. Sullivan loved the high life and spent his money faster than he earned it. Rachel sought to set his cultural target: 'Will you let Gounod carry off the palm? You have the tools all ready – you have the prizes before you . . . will you win for yourself a name and a place among the great men who have gone before?'

Rachel was wary of Sullivan's tendency to turn a quick fiver by writing to the popular level of demand, as in his spate of parlour ballads and hymns. His *Cox and Box* and *The Contrabandista* (both 1867) were pieces of unadulterated fun which mark his entry to the comedy theatre; yet such was her infatuation with Sullivan the man that she went to *Cox and Box* and 'enjoyed it greatly', and she helped Sullivan copy and correct the score of *The Contrabandista*. But to the musical academics of London it was shocking that their Great White Hope should turn to this sort of thing. The historical importance of these two musical farces, however, was considerable, in that a gifted and classically trained composer had entered a field which had for a century been the bawdy hunting-ground of hacks and mediocrities.

Cox and Box was initially no more than a lark suggested by F. C. Burnand (later editor of *Punch*) who was getting up a musical supper-party at his home; he had the idea of entertaining his friends with Maddison Morton's farce *Box and Cox* turned into a musical. Sullivan agreed to write the music, the title was reversed, and within a few days the party was held at midnight, attended by many actors who had come on from their theatres. Box was played by George du Maurier, actor, artist and future author of *Trilby*. Such parties were a feature of artistic London. This one was such a riot that a second presentation was demanded at Moray Lodge, Kensington. This was the exquisite home of Arthur Lewis, head of a Regent Street millinery firm, who was himself a talented painter. His wife was Kate Terry, sister of the great Ellen; his grandsons are Sir John Gielgud and Val Gielgud. Bohemian nights at Moray Lodge attracted men as varied as Trollope and Tattersall the horse-dealer. Arthur Sullivan, pounding away his accompaniment at the piano, thoroughly enjoyed the cigar-smoking company, and his tit-bit made such an impression on them that a charity repeat was organized by the Moray Minstrels, as they called themselves. Sullivan orchestrated his music,

George Grove, later knighted on the same day as Sullivan and the composer's great friend. An important figure in the musical world of his time, he is today remembered as the originator and editor of *Grove's Dictionary of Music and Musicians*.

F. C. Burnand, the dramatist and later editor of *Punch*, who stimulated Sullivan to write the music for *Cox and Box*.

(*Left*) Invitation to a party at Moray Lodge, 1865. The Moray Minstrels might include such diverse figures as Thackeray, Trollope, Millais, Lord Leighton and Tattersall.

(*Below*) Playbill for *Cox and Box* at Thomas German Reed's Royal Gallery of Illustration.

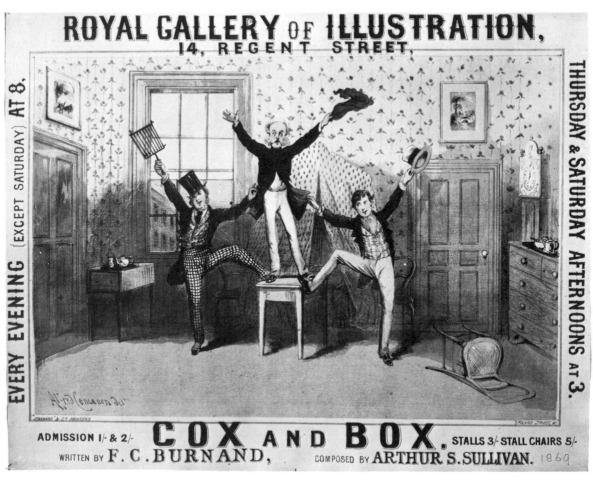

and on 11 May 1867 the curtain at the Adelphi Theatre rose on the first
public performance of a Sullivan comedy.

Thomas German Reed immediately bought the performing rights and
presented *Cox and Box* at his Royal Gallery of Illustration in Lower Regent
Street, a place of chaste entertainment for that section of the respectable
Victorian public which would never on any account visit a 'theatre' – hence
the camouflaged name. Uniquely, German Reed had not floated on the
wave of theatrical vulgarity; now, a small-scale composer himself, he
recognized the large-scale promise in Sullivan.

A critic from *Fun* was also present at the Adelphi, one W.S. Gilbert:
'Mr Sullivan's music is, in many places, of too high a class for the grotesquely
absurd plot to which it is wedded. It is very funny, here and there, and grand
or graceful where it is not funny; but the grand and the graceful have, we
think, too large a share of the honours to themselves.' This criticism is
a remarkable foretaste of the disagreements which were to dog the Gilbert-
Sullivan partnership of later years.

Emboldened to widen his public, German Reed quickly commissioned
Sullivan and Burnand to write a larger piece, *The Contrabandista*; he hired an
orchestra of forty players, and aspired to mount it more lavishly than the

View of Piccadilly Circus in 1842,
the year of Sullivan's birth. The
Royal Gallery of Illustration is just
visible on the left-hand side of
Regent Street, on the far side of the
Circus.

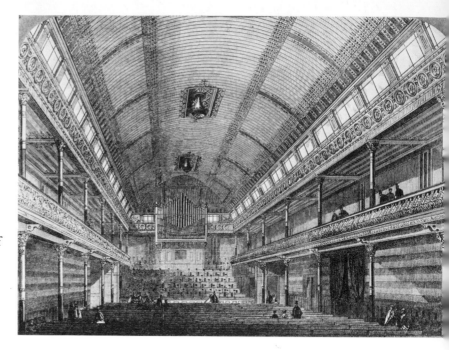

St George's Opera House (St George's Hall), scene of the failure of Sullivan's first comic opera, *The Contrabandista*. Much later the building became the BBC's chief light entertainment studio in London, until it was destroyed in the Blitz in 1940.

miniatures at the Royal Gallery of Illustration, so he took a lease on the new St George's Hall (close to the present site of Broadcasting House) and re-named it St George's Opera House. Hitherto there had been such a dearth of English composers that most *opéra bouffe* was imported from France, where Offenbach was its king, but in 'adapting' these works for the English stage the Gallic naughtinesses were cut out and replaced by all the shoddy stock-in-hand of the English stage: puns, clumsy innuendoes, men dressed as women, women as men, feeble singing, slatternly acting. Any delicate Gallic spice which remained seemed to weather badly its transportation into the strange foreign atmosphere of an England where prudishness and vulgarity flourished side by side. German Reed's challenge to this French predominance failed. The British public was not yet ready for the higher level of his musical theatre. Takings did not cover expenses, so the orchestra was dismissed and *The Contrabandista* was replaced by *Cox and Box*, its accompaniment reduced to a piano and a harmonium. It ran for some three hundred performances.

To Sullivan these productions were merely jocular 'asides' to the main flow of his music. In this same critical year of 1867, he was writing orchestral and chamber music, urged on by the unremitting Rachel, and his gentle setting of Sir Walter Scott's 'O Hush Thee, My Babie' won lasting renown. He went on a Continental tour, visited his student haunts at Leipzig (where he conducted *In Memoriam*), and in Vienna with his close friend George Grove made musical history. It seems likely that during this tour Sullivan first had the idea of writing an oratorio on the parable of the Prodigal Son; Biblical oratorio was what England expected of Sullivan, and he expected it of himself – a Mendelssohn Scholar to follow in the steps of Mendelssohn, not to mention Handel; yet the fact is that posterity was to be enriched not by *The Prodigal Son* (never performed now) but by the two Englishmen's discovery of many Schubert manuscripts long lost in Viennese cupboards: three immortal symphonies, at least forty unpublished songs, and the full score of the superb *Rosamunde* music. Sullivan and Grove, enthusiastic for the little-recognized Schubert, thought this a wonderful event, as indeed it was, for on returning to London they organized concerts which brought Schubert back from obscurity.

For Sullivan the tour was a refreshment at the founts of classical music. How thrilled he was to meet an aged clerk who had attended Schubert's christening and to visit the Mozartium at Salzburg, how awed to stand at the graves of Beethoven and Schubert! What an inspiration 'to be prolific, darling, like the great men before you', as Rachel wrote! But Sullivan's travels impressed him also in quite another direction. He took a party of English glee-singers to appear at the 1867 Paris Exhibition, and while Sullivan was worthily attending to his duties there Offenbach's comic opera *The Grand Duchess* was the talk of the city. Sullivan would not have been Sullivan had he ignored its gaiety and musicianship. Offenbach was writing comic opera in the idiom of France, he was making the people laugh and sing, and earning a fortune. Then on to Vienna: while Sullivan was earnestly searching there for the Schubert manuscripts he heard on every side the

Hortense Schneider in the title-role in Offenbach's *The Grand Duchess*.

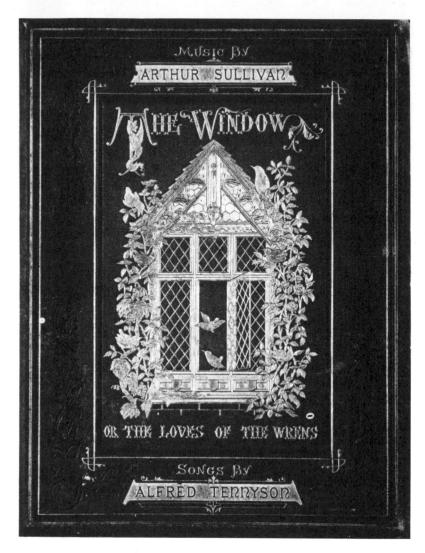

The cover of *The Window, or the Loves of the Wrens*, Sullivan's setting of some of Tennyson's poems. Tennyson felt the verses 'are too light and will damage his reputation', Sullivan confided to his mother.

waltzes of Johann Strauss the Second, soon to move on to *Die Fledermaus*; Strauss too was writing in the idiom of his people, the Viennese, with an emphasis on the gaiety rather than the earnestness of life. If Offenbach and Strauss, why not Sullivan? What about the idiom of England? Sullivan could do with the money. If *The Prodigal Son*, why not comic operas as well? These thoughts, this philosophy of plurality, lay behind his work from now onwards. He was pulled in many directions. Back in England, he was attracted to the prestige of a long-standing scheme of George Grove's that Sullivan should join Tennyson and Millais in a volume of music, verse and art. Grove and Sullivan had already visited the Poet Laureate at his house in the Isle of Wight where Sullivan played on 'a very tinkly piano' (said Grove) and Tennyson recited into the early hours. Millais did some pencil sketches, but later dropped out, while Tennyson so lost faith in his own verses that he called them 'quite silly' and tried to stop publication by offering £500 compensation. Sullivan refused, and *The Window, or the Loves of the Wrens* was eventually published with an apologetic preface by Tennyson.

When Gilbert turned to Tennyson for inspiration, as he did at about the same time, it was not for prestige but for parody. He had begun to show his stature as a playwright and decided to experiment in blank verse, so he parodied Tennyson's *Princess*. 'A picturesque story', he called his version, 'told in a strain of mock-heroic seriousness.' Here was the basic recipe for most future Gilbertian opera, the mock-heroic (in point of fact *The Princess* was later transformed into *Princess Ida*). In his parody play of 1870 Gilbert included lyrics sung to already existing tunes, as was the custom in old-style ballad operas such as *The Beggar's Opera*. His need was for a composer as original as himself.

Mr Gilbert was first introduced to Mr Sullivan in 1869 by the composer Frederic Clay during a rehearsal of Clay's operetta *Ages Ago*, with words by Gilbert, at the Royal Gallery of Illustration: they had a brief banter, then the two men who were to become the greatest partnership in the history of English entertainment parted with no designs on one another. Their paths merely crossed and diverged. Sullivan, a squat fellow of twenty-seven years of age, beautifully dressed in frock-coat and tall hat, with glossy black hair, an eyeglass and a jaunty manner, was soon to conduct his *Prodigal Son* at Worcester. Some people said this would thrust him to the top of the musical tree. Gilbert, aged thirty-three, a giant with bristling eyebrows and the brusque manner of an anglicized mikado, was half-way up the theatrical tree, and rising fast. The stage at Mr Reed's modest Gallery served to try out his ideas. In *Ages Ago* the animation of ancestral portraits hanging in a manorial hall anticipated *Ruddigore*; his *No Cards* included a foretaste of *Patience*; and *Our Island Home* (music by Thomas German Reed) had vestiges of both *The Pirates of Penzance* and *H.M.S. Pinafore*. To quote an old pun, Gilbertian opera was cradled among the Reeds.

Gilbert's doodle to illustrate the 'cradled among the Reeds' pun.

For Sullivan *The Prodigal Son* had hung fire. When he got round to it he knocked out this oratorio in a few breakneck weeks, to Rachel's ecstatic satisfaction: '*The Prodigal* is too beautiful and it made me weep to read it. I want you to conduct from my copy – will you? I should like it, and I will try to do it beautifully and will make as few mistakes as possible.'

The first performance was at the Three Choirs Festival in Worcester, where a small boy named Edward Elgar, aged twelve, was living. It was Elgar, not Sullivan, who was to raise English oratorio to new and enduring heights (with *The Dream of Gerontius*, 1900); but after the 1869 *Prodigal Son* everyone sang Sullivan's praises, though Sir John Goss wrote: 'All you have done is most masterly. Some day you will, I hope, try at another oratorio, putting out all your strength – not the strength of a few weeks or months. Show yourself the best man in Europe! Don't do anything so pretentious as an oratorio or even a symphony without *all your power* which seldom comes in one fit.' Sullivan was himself appointed a Royal Academy of Music professor in this year.

The entire story of the wreckage of the Rachel-Arthur idyll is not known; Sullivan's side of the correspondence seems to have been destroyed (possibly burnt by Rachel) while her letters, ribbon-tied in a bundle, he kept to his

Arthur Sullivan: 'There are so many things I want to do for music, if God will give me two days for every one in which to do them' (from a letter to his mother).

death. A musician who vacillated between oratorio and comic operetta, of all vulgar things, did not impress Mr Scott Russell. The young people were forbidden to meet. Rachel's letters became first clandestine ('If when you get this you want to see me dreadfully I will go to the rockery at $\frac{1}{2}$ past 3'), then distraught ('My whole nature revolts against this pain'), but two such temperaments as hers and Sullivan's were almost sure to clash. She bickered about his 'going out to miserable sickly London parties, smoking half the night through'. Her devotion to his 'genius' could be overbearing: 'I want you now at once to re-write your violoncello concerto, there are beautiful things in it but it is incomplete and unequal. I insist.' In 1869 she wrote her farewell: 'With all my heart I thank you for the past which has given colour to my life.' Three years later she married a civil servant who took her to India – where she died of cholera when only thirty-seven.

One can judge a man to some extent by his women. On the eve of one of Sullivan's visits to Paris a letter from Rachel lectures him at one end on the evils of the Gay City, and is frivolous at the other: 'I want you to get me three pairs of cool cotton stockings – coloured – which will wash well. Are

W. S. Gilbert: 'For, look you, there is humour in all things, and the truest philosophy is that which teaches us to find it and to make the most of it' (Jack Point, in *The Yeomen of the Guard*).

you answered? Blue I like best.' Compare Gilbert in Paris; he spent the day working in his hotel room, then wrote to his Dearest Kits: 'I don't much like being a bachelor. . . . I have bought some chocolate to console myself with. I wish you were here, old girl.'

In the early 1870s Gilbert was established as a front-rank author of both serious and comic plays; he prospered financially, notably through *Pygmalion and Galatea* (1871), in which the lovely Mrs Kendal played Galatea, the statue that comes to life. With its subsequent revivals this play earned him £40,000. Affluence brought the Gilberts' removal to a sizable house in The Boltons, South Kensington. A neighbour was the distinguished singer Jenny Lind. We get an amusing glimpse of the Gilberts' domestic life in *Kitty's Cookery Book*, a collection of her recipes which Lady Gilbert published in 1914. On the title-page is a couplet of distinctive Gilbertian flavour: 'A Thing of Beauty is a Joy for Ever, Especially a Cook Who's Clean and Clever.' The recipes show that they ate such foods as Jenny Lind Soup, Curzon Street Gingerbread (W.S.G. had courted Kitten in Curzon Street), and Religious Cod (for Fridays?).

Cartoon by 'Ape' of Alfred, Duke of Edinburgh, a close friend of Sullivan and a prominent patron of music.

Mrs Gilbert was the complete mistress of the household as staff increased. She had no offspring, but children's parties at The Boltons were famed for W.S.G.'s boisterousness and Kitty's food. His business friends, too, were given more than 'Religious Cod'. His dominating figure had become well known about town, not in Sullivan's musical circles but in the theatres and in clubland: he had joined the Savage Club in 1864 (subscription £1 a year). His mordant manner launched a hundred chestnuts. Leaving the Haymarket Theatre one night he was accosted by a man who mistook him for an attendant, provoking the following exchange: 'Hey! You!' 'You talking to me, sir?' 'Yes,' said the stranger, 'Call me a cab.' 'Certainly. You're a four-wheeler.' 'How dare you, sir! What do you mean?' 'You asked me to call you a cab, and I couldn't call you "hansom".'

German Reed tried to unite Gilbert and Sullivan professionally, but by now Sullivan was fishing profitably in grander waters than the Royal Gallery of Illustration. He had a great success with his *Overture di Ballo*, first performed at the Birmingham Festival of 1870, a scintillating piece of orchestral gaiety. In the same year Sullivan was writing ballads, hymn-tunes, a cantata for the International Exhibition and some carols, among them 'It came upon the midnight clear'. He was conducting up and down the country. Queen Victoria commanded that a complete set of his works be sent to Windsor, and she asked him to edit the amateur compositions of Prince Albert. A strong friendship had been formed between Sullivan and the Queen's second son, Prince Alfred, Duke of Edinburgh, who was a genuine lover of music. The boy from Lambeth had gone far. He was receiving £400 a year as a retainer from Boosey the publisher for the publishing rights of his works, on top of his substantial royalties.

Such excellent music as *di Ballo* and such plays as Gilbert's best in this period were tokens of the change towards a more elegant style which was coming over English artistic life in general. John Ruskin, Slade Professor at Oxford, at the height of his fame, was preaching the gospel of Beauty. The aesthetic school took root (later to be parodied in *Patience*). Pre-Raphaelite artists were painting Beauty as they saw it, meticulous paintings 'true to Nature', often with a 'message'. Lewis Carroll was publishing *Alice Through the Looking Glass*, with its charming illustrations by Tenniel. A spirit of political change was also in the air. The wind of rebellion blew across the Channel, that fierce wind of the 1870/71 Revolution which made France a Republic and sent Napoleon III flying to England with his Empress Eugénie. The wind moderated as it reached the cliffs of Dover, yet even there a breeze of change was blowing the cobwebs away. The Education Act of 1870 provided that all children must have an elementary education. W.S. Gilbert himself became the agent of change in the theatre. He was determined to see his plays presented with taste and vigour, so he now began throwing his weight about as producer, as well as author. By autocratic, hard-hitting methods he set about demolishing the turgid traditions of the Victorian stage, against the resistance of players who could not fathom why an author should have a say in their interpretation of what he had written. From Gilbert's new eminence he could challenge the entrenched position of the most eminent of stars – Mrs Kendall's Galatea, for example, did not escape his caustic

correction. Rehearsing one play after another, it was a stubborn process of education, of repetition upon repetition until he was satisfied not only with the movements and articulation of the players but with the scenery, lighting, costumes – the whole had to seem cohesive to his eagle eye. This was Gilbert's revolution, and he next carried it into the slapdash and pornographic musical theatre.

In 1871 John Hollingshead at the Gaiety Theatre received the script of Gilbert's 'entirely original grotesque Opera in two acts', *Thespis*. He sent it to Sullivan, who at once agreed to compose the music, a decision which probably surprised Hollingshead as much as it elevated the eyebrows of London's musical intelligentsia. Sullivan's experience earlier that year in providing incidental music for *The Merchant of Venice* at the Prince's Theatre, Manchester, perhaps fomented anew his innate sense of theatre; certainly he found *Thespis* to be 'entirely original'. It was packed with Gilbertianisms such as the Chairman of Directors of the North, South, East, West Diddlesex Junction Railway who was 'conspicuous exceeding, for his happy way and easy breeding':

(*Left*) Lucy Gilbert, whose self-effacing charm contributed much to the success of her happy though childless marriage. She died, aged eighty-six, in 1936. (*Right*) The Gilberts' comfortable home at 24 The Boltons, a quiet backwater in Kensington. F. C. Burnand and the famous singers Madame Albani and Jenny Lind lived in the same distinguished street.

Thespis in rehearsal at the Gaiety Theatre, December 1871. The author can be seen peering out from behind the gas 'T-piece'.

Each Christmas Day he gave each stoker
A silver shovel and a golden poker,
And he'd button-hole flowers for the ticket sorters
And rich Bath-buns for the outside porters. . . .

This is a single sparkling bubble in Gilbert's champagne of English nonsense and to understand the failure of the 1871 vintage we have to bear in mind the context of that period: *Thespis* was a satirical send-up of a mythological theme, set on Mount Olympus. Only an educated man could have distilled it. Sullivan recognized its quality and he knew Offenbach's classical romp *Orpheus in the Underworld* from productions in Paris and London; he may have wished to be the English Bach but he could not resist an opportunity to be the English Offenbach as well.

Sullivan's own sense of fun was shown in such touches as his weaving of a railway bell and whistle into his orchestration of the Diddlesex Junction ditty; more important, *Thespis* was unusual in having completely original – not borrowed – music. The *Daily Telegraph* considered that the music was 'quite in character with the author's design'. In fact both Sullivan and Gilbert were well fitted by training and disposition to team up as revolutionaries in the English musical theatre. Yet *Thespis* flopped; it has never been seen since, and it can never be seen again because all the music has disappeared, except one song, 'Little Maid of Arcadee', which was published as a separate ballad, and one chorus, 'Climbing over Rocky Mountain', which was served up again in *The Pirates of Penzance*.

There were other reasons for the *Thespis* collapse. It had less than one week's rehearsal. 'Crude and ineffective', snorted Gilbert. Sullivan, who conducted the first performance on 26 December 1871, told his mother that musically the performance was 'rather bad'. Under-rehearsal suggests that neither Sullivan nor Gilbert had foreseen what a daunting task was before them. Gilbert, as producer, sought to introduce discipline and new ideas. He drilled the reluctant stars severely and tried to animate the chorus, hitherto 'nothing more than the stage-setting,' as Sullivan put it.

The *Sporting Life*'s critic complained that *Thespis* was over people's heads and this journalist knew what he was talking about. At the Gaiety, known chiefly as a burlesque house, the scene on Mount Olympus was a dead loss. Hollingshead's stock burlesque company failed to strike the subtle Gilbertian style of mock-serious comedy acting. The least enslaved to Gaiety traditions was Fred Sullivan, the composer's brother, architect turned actor, and hence not a Gaiety stereotype. He played Apollo. The piece dragged on. 'It was past midnight when the curtain descended', reported *Punch*, 'and the audience was in a fidgety state to get away.' During January box-office takings waned,

Cartoon of John Hollingshead. A showman ahead of his time, he built the Gaiety in an attempt to improve on the 'dirty and defective' state of the average London theatre.

A scene from the first performance of *Thespis*.

despite a visit by the Duke of Edinburgh, and *Thespis* closed at the end of the month.

Lessons were learned. Gilbert made public his caustic opinion of the skimped rehearsal system (in *Tom Hood's Comic Annual*, 1873); in future he and Sullivan were to hand-pick their casts without regard to famous stars, but they had no such precognitions when they parted early in 1872, for they had neither plans nor dreams of further co-operation in the theatre. During the next three years each paddled his own canoe, in opposite directions. Gilbert steered an erratic public course from a play, daring for its day, called *Charity* (about the Victorian 'fallen woman') to the sentimental *Sweethearts* and a French farce which he translated in a day and a half to earn £2,500. His private course was collision-prone with litigation over his rights and tart letters over other people's wrongs, yet we know from correspondence that Gilbert privately helped many a lame dog over a stile.

In the same three years Arthur Sullivan followed a smooth, swift, and unswerving course. He collided with no one. He made the music that England wanted, and that music made him the bard of the people and the friend of princes. When the Prince of Wales recovered from typhoid fever it was Sullivan who was called upon to write a *Te Deum* for a mammoth public rejoicing at the Crystal Palace, with two thousand performers. It had a triumph excelled only by his second oratorio *The Light of the World*, first performed in 1873 at Birmingham. Queen Victoria said: '*The Light of the World* is destined to uplift British music.' This remark assured Sullivan's position as the laureate of English 'serious' music. In Birmingham one day, Manchester the next, travelling, conducting, he composed over twenty of his popular ballads in these years, and twice as many hymns. The Society for Propagating Christian Knowledge made Sullivan editor of their Hymnal. He even became Musical Director of the Royal Westminster Aquarium (opposite Westminster Abbey) which offered Londoners a combination of live fish and lively music.

Academically, he was appointed professor at the Crystal Palace School. With other musicians he held a watching brief over the operation of the Education Act of 1870 to ensure that an elementary schooling should not exclude class-singing. He week-ended at the Duke of Edinburgh's Eastwell Park in Kent, playing piano duets with the Duke's fiancée, the daughter of Tsar Alexander II of Russia. He cultivated Napoleon III and his Empress, now exiled in England. His only connection with the stage in these years was when John Hollingshead asked him to compose incidental music for *The Merry Wives of Windsor* at the Gaiety. As with *The Tempest* a dozen years earlier, Sullivan responded to Shakespeare's Englishness with songs and dances in the deep, clear stream of English music – a quality which Sullivan, having hardly a drop of English blood in his veins, acquired from study and love of the subject rather than by inheritance (Gilbert, by contrast, disliked Shakespeare). Hollingshead exploited the box-office 'pull' of Sullivan-Shakespeare, but after the disastrous *Thespis* he had no use for Sullivan-Gilbert. Indeed, with Sullivan at the top of the 'serious' musical tree it now needed an exceptionally powerful human catalyst to fuse together such (at first sight) dissimilar qualities: that of Richard D'Oyly Carte.

HYMN 9

The service due to GOD
Is not mere babbling words.
Pour'd tunefully upon the ear
Like songs of singing birds.

The service due to GOD
Is no mere formal part,
'Tis not enough to bow the head,
And never bow the heart!

The service due to GOD
Is life from evil won,
And faith and hope and glowing love,
And duly bravely done.

Strong Help of feeble faith,
Pure guide of age and youth,
Teach us to serve THEE, holy GOD,
In spirit and in truth.

A page from a children's hymnal for which Sullivan arranged the music.

Richard D'Oyly Carte, a man of wide culture and exceptional organizing ability whose family have continued to foster and guard the Gilbert and Sullivan tradition. His friendship with Sullivan became close, with Gilbert markedly less so.

In 1875 Carte was thirty-one and manager of Madame Selina Dolaro's small Royalty Theatre in Soho, where on 25 March the curtain went up on the piece which soundly established Gilbert and Sullivan opera as a perfect art – for *Trial by Jury* is nothing less, a superlative gem that flashes as sharply today as when it was first produced. It is the only Gilbert and Sullivan work with no spoken dialogue; it is the shortest of the lot – less than forty minutes. There's not a solemn gesture in it, and yet its subject is one of the most solemn that Gilbert could have chosen, the British system of justice. He takes a look back at his own days at the Bar, and presents a case for breach of promise of marriage on a level of genial (not sour) satire which is caught superbly by Sullivan's music from its first bar to the finale when the Judge, bedevilled by barristers and bewitched by the plaintiff, tosses his papers about, singing 'Put your briefs upon the shelf, I will marry her myself!'

Carte was much more than a shrewd executive, he was also a fastidious musician: he had himself composed operettas for St George's Hall and the

Opéra Comique before he met Gilbert and Sullivan. This combination of qualities was the key to Carte's catalyst function, and to the friendship that was to grow up between him and Sullivan, rather than with Gilbert. The D'Oyly Cartes were a Soho family, of ancestry crossing Norman blood (1066, D'Oyly) with Welsh (Jones). They were so devoted to Gallic culture that when Richard was a boy French was spoken in the home two days a week. His father (also Richard) was a professional flautist and partner in a musical instrument firm. Music was the Cartes' pleasure and their business. A love of pictorial art, French and English, was also given to the boy who in later years was to be the friend of Whistler and the patron of 'forward' movements in art.

He was educated at University School and after a spell in his father's business set up his own theatrical and lecture agency off the Charing Cross Road. About 1869 he began evolving his favourite idea: 'The starting of English comic opera in a theatre devoted to that alone was the scheme of my life', he wrote later. In 1870 he suggested it to Sullivan, in 1874 to both Gilbert and Sullivan – 'but it fell through because I was short of money.'

Early in the following year Carte was at the Royalty Theatre, looking glumly at the box-office returns. *La Périchole* was by the ever-popular Offenbach, but it was rather short as an evening's entertainment; Carte was looking for a curtain-raiser to fill the bill, something very English and just as gay as Offenbach. His problem was solved by a splendid coincidence of fortuity and foresight.

The fortuitous happening was that Gilbert walked in that day, Carte mentioned his need of a fill-up, and W.S.G. instantly offered him a breach of promise case. Some five years previously, he explained, *Fun* had published a Bab Ballad called *Trial by Jury*, and recently he had expanded it into a musical mock trial with the idea of Carl Rosa (impresario of grand opera) writing the music and his wife, Euphrosyne Parepa-Rosa, appearing in the lead.

The foresight came from Carte: Sullivan, he said, should compose, not Carl Rosa. He remembered the lamented *Thespis*; he discerned that failure was not a write-off for Gilbert and Sullivan opera, but rather a promise. At his behest Gilbert took his script to Sullivan's rooms. Over a blazing fire, Sullivan recalled, 'he read it through to me in a perturbed sort of way with a gradual crescendo of indignation, in the manner of a man considerably disappointed with what he had written. As soon as he had come to the last word he closed up the manuscript violently, apparently unconscious of the fact that he had achieved his purpose.' Sullivan wrote the music in a fortnight.

The first-night critics were almost unanimous in praise, topped by *The Times*: 'It seems, as in the great Wagnerian operas, as though poem and music had proceeded simultaneously from one and the same brain.' True, the *Musical Times* observed pompously that 'the versatile composer of *The Light of the World* has turned his attention lately to musical burlesque', but discerning music-lovers delighted in Sullivan's fresh adroitness, and chortled at such clever parodies as the jurymen's salute to the judge in Handelian style, and the florid spoofing of Italian grand opera. The man in the gallery found he could enjoy it, too. The whole show was stuffed with tunes you could

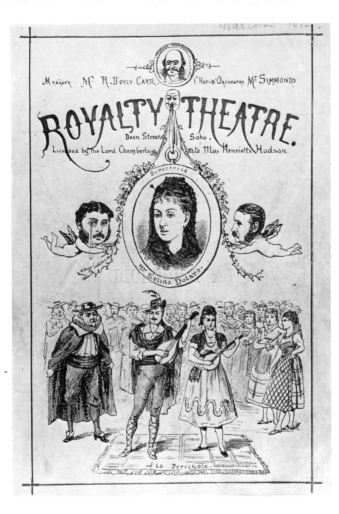

D'Oyly Carte's programme for
La Périchole and *Trial by Jury*.

whistle. And well dressed. The girls good to look at. Best of all, *Trial by Jury*
turned on that love of ridiculing their betters and national institutions which is
a healthy English safety-valve. This new kind of opera was ridiculous, and
yet it was not rubbish. As entertainment it was far more intelligent than any of
its rivals.

The quintessence of Gilbert and Sullivan is that they can be both ridiculous
and intelligent at the same time. The great significance of their *Trial by Jury*
was that it marked the re-awakening of English comic opera, almost dormant
for a hundred and fifty years. Like *The Beggar's Opera* of 1728, all Gilbert
and Sullivan opera is thoroughly native in subject, words and music. The
French paramountcy on the English stage was ended: *La Périchole* soon disappeared from the Royalty and the piece commissioned as a fill-up became,
by its unmatched sparkle and wit, a focus of admiration in London (except
for the Lord Chief Justice, who thought it was calculated to bring the Bench
into contempt). *Trial by Jury* enjoyed a total run of 200 performances at
the Royalty, Opéra Comique and Strand theatres in turn (1875–77).

The success of this operetta and its followers profoundly influenced better
standards of taste and performance on the British stage, and the Gilbert-

Edward, Prince of Wales; Sullivan became one of 'the playboy Prince's' boon companions and frequently entertained him at his rooms.

Sullivan-Carte renaissance was itself influenced in a wider sense by the improving standards of education among the general public. The 1870 Education Act was having gradual but great effects. Women were emerging from the strict confines of the Victorian home: in the year of *Trial by Jury* Newnham College for women was founded at Cambridge, and in the previous year Girton had begun; as more women – educated women – began to go to the theatre they influenced its standards. Again, parallel with the Gilbert-Carte advance in scenery and costume design there was a wider aesthetic crusade led by William Morris, the artist and craftsman who in 1871 (the year of *Thespis*) had bought Kelmscott, the lovely manor-house near Lechlade, and started the Kelmscott Press which became a symbol of good design. Morris set new standards in book production, in furniture, in dress design, in the colour and texture of materials, all of which were to have repercussions on the stage, and to all of which Gilbert, Sullivan and Carte were actively sympathetic.

Landmark as we now recognize *Trial by Jury* to have been, the revolutionaries did not move on promptly to new conquests. Gilbert and Carl Rosa were still contemplating a collaboration, which might have robbed posterity of much. Sullivan relaxed at Cadenabbia on Lake Como with his aristocratic friends. 'It is all very beautiful and sweetly lazy,' he wrote to his mother. Returning, he took up the directorship of the Glasgow Orpheus Choir. With his old friend the Duke of Edinburgh and his new friend the Prince of Wales he discussed the foundation of a National Training School of Music, and it was duly founded in 1876 with Sullivan as principal (he held the post until 1881). This is now the Royal College of Music. Sullivan wrote to Mum: 'There are so many things I want to do for music if God will only give me two days for every one in which to do them.'

D'Oyly Carte tried to bring Gilbert and Sullivan together again by suggesting that they write a full-length comic opera, but it was not so easy to get this prancing pair to respond. Gilbert was producing his *Engaged* at the Haymarket with his favourite Marion Terry in the lead, and his *Broken Hearts* at the Court Theatre was W.S.G.'s pet play.

Sullivan was high-stepping in another direction, as a letter from Cambridge shows: 'Dearest Mum. The deed is done and I am Mus.Doc. Now I am dressed in a black silk gown (evening dress) and a trencher hat and am going to dine in hall at my own college (Trinity) and then go for an evening party at the Master's.' Three years later Oxford followed. Gilbert was never awarded an honorary degree (his knighthood, too, was to be delayed twenty-four years after Sullivan's).

Despite the distinctions showered upon him, Sullivan was never conceited or unapproachable. A student of music later renowned as Sir Landon Ronald aspired to compose an operetta and ventured to seek 'the great man's' advice on orchestration: 'He asked me if I was going to the next Richter concert. I replied in the affirmative. "Well," he said, "the wonderful Mozart symphony in G minor is being performed. Go and buy a pianoforte copy of it. Take it with you to the concert, listen well to the orchestration, and the next morning score it yourself from the pianoforte copy. Then go and buy Mozart's full score, compare it with yours, and you'll learn much."'

44

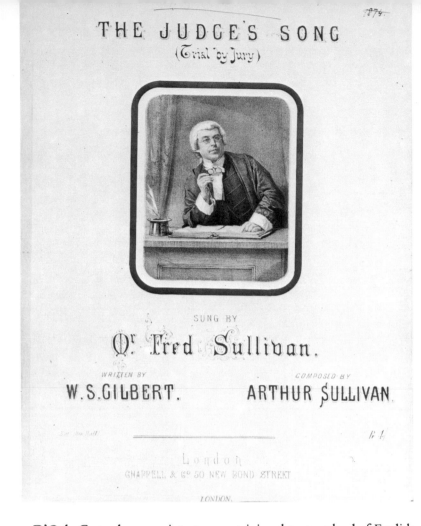

THE JUDGE'S SONG

(Trial by Jury)

SUNG BY

Mr Fred Sullivan.

WRITTEN BY
W.S.GILBERT.

COMPOSED BY
ARTHUR SULLIVAN.

London
CHAPPELL & C° 50 NEW BOND STREET

LONDON.

Fred Sullivan as the Judge in *Trial by Jury*.

D'Oyly Carte alone was intent on sustaining the new school of English light opera: he suggested a revival of *Thespis* with revised script and music. Sullivan and Gilbert agreed, provided that Carte would guarantee a hundred performances at a fee of two guineas a night for each of them, the fees for fifty nights to be paid in advance. A month later Gilbert wrote to Sullivan: 'I have heard no more about *Thespis*. It's astonishing how quickly these capitalists dry up under the magic influence of the words "cash down".' But Carte, the would-be capitalist, was genuinely finding it hard to finance a production on the artistic scale that he, and they, would wish to present after the success of *Trial by Jury*; he therefore recruited four pukka capitalists (one of them, known as 'Water-cart Bailey', held the monopoly in spraying the streets of London); with himself as Managing Director they constituted the Comedy Opera Company.

The run of *Trial by Jury* had meanwhile been brought to an untimely end when Fred Sullivan – whose superlatively Gilbertian playing of the Judge was acclaimed the acting 'hit' of the show – died at the age of thirty-nine. During a vigil at Fred's bedside Arthur had been moved to write that piece of solemn Victoriana 'The Lost Chord', which soon became the most hackneyed

George Grossmith as John Wellington Wells in *The Sorcerer*. Gilbert
and Sullivan opera raised him to
stardom; he also, with his brother
Weedon, wrote the immortal *Diary
of a Nobody* (1892).

ballad of the century and which by contrast with anything in the con-
temporaneous *Trial by Jury* illustrates where his true musical genius lay.

When a new opera by Dr Sullivan and Mr Gilbert appeared, in November
1877, it was *The Sorcerer*, the Comedy Opera Company having leased the
Opéra Comique theatre in a slummy labyrinth near the Strand, and paid the
collaborators an advance of two hundred guineas. For the first time they were
complete masters of casting, rehearsal and décor; Carte saw to that. They
founded a new school of acting by casting to their own unusual perceptions,
disregarding the merits of West End stardom; in due course their recruits
became the distinctive stars of Savoy Opera. George Grossmith, for instance,
was a minor entertainer at provincial working men's clubs when he was
called to an audition for the part of John Wellington Wells, partner in a
nineteenth-century City firm of 'Family Sorcerers'. Modest little Grossmith
said to Gilbert: 'For the part of a magician I should have thought you required
a fine man with a fine voice.' Gilbert replied, 'That is exactly what we don't
want.' In defiance of a telegram to Carte from Water-cart Bailey and his

pettifogging capitalists – 'Whatever you do don't engage Grossmith' – Grossmith was engaged.

On the opening night Grossmith was an instant success, whisking blithely round the stage with his absurd tea-pot full of love-potion. Gilbert's weakness for elixirs of love and magic lozenges was to bedevil his relations with Sullivan much later but it appeared in *The Sorcerer* with such success that the *Observer*'s judgment on the opera – 'masterly' – was backed almost unanimously by the critics and within a week Sullivan wrote to a friend: 'We are doing tremendous business at the Op. Comique I am glad to say . . . another nail in the coffin of Opéra Bouffe from the French!' Indeed, the historical importance of *The Sorcerer* is that in it Sullivan no longer parodies other composers: its music is truly creative Anglo-Sullivan. And now Sullivan of Lambeth began to taste the full rewards of his creativity, leasing a swagger apartment in Albert Mansions, Westminster.

Princess Louise, daughter of Queen Victoria, heads the list of guests at a party given by Sullivan at this time. Even more significantly, they include Mrs

The Sorcerer at the Opéra Comique. Wells pours love philtre into a tea-pot in a scene described by the review which accompanied this drawing as 'a rich burlesque on some operatic incantations'.

Part of a letter from Sullivan to his mother listing the guests expected at one of his parties.

(*Right*) Mrs Ronalds (born Mary Frances Carter of Boston), Sullivan's intimate friend and one of the few people permitted to call informally on the Prince and Princess of Wales: 'I would travel the length of my kingdom to hear Mrs Ronalds sing "The Lost Chord",' said the Prince.

Mary Ronalds, a rich, gifted and beautiful American who had separated from her husband ten years earlier and had settled at 7 Cadogan Place where she held Sunday evening 'musicales' attended by the rich and the musical; she was herself an attractive singer. She was dubbed 'the permanent ambassadress of the United States at the Court of St James', having become a much-favoured member of the Prince of Wales's set, and as such she met Sullivan. Perusal of Sullivan's diary suggests from the timing of his private appointments at Cadogan Place and the curious symbols he used that she was his mistress. Such was the discretion of these two, however, who were seen together on public occasions yet never raised a whisper of scandal, that Mrs Ronalds remains a rather mysterious creature. In Victoria's reign so respected a figure as Sullivan was perforce discreet or his career in serious music would have been shattered; divorce and remarriage with Mrs Ronalds were likewise prevented by this taboo as much as by her husband's reluctance to take action. Pierre Ronalds only filed a petition for divorce in 1900, the year of Sullivan's death; he later withdrew it. Without a doubt Mrs Ronalds was Sullivan's chief confidante for over twenty years. In the diary she figures as 'Mrs R'. Other initials (as in 'Wrote letters to L.W., Mother, and the Duke of

Edinburgh') may well represent 'Little Woman' and refer to her also. When Mrs Ronalds died in 1916 Sullivan's original manuscript of 'The Lost Chord' was buried in her grave at Brompton Cemetery.

In 1878 when Mrs Ronalds was thirty-nine years of age, Sullivan wrote to Mum: 'The party at Marlborough House was very small and very swell. The Prince and Princess were both very kind to me and Mrs Ronalds sang "The Lost Chord" splendidly.' One of the few Gilbert diaries that survives is of this year, when he was preparing the next opera, *H.M.S. Pinafore*; it could scarcely reveal a home life in greater contrast to Sullivan's. Its scrappy entries give glimpses of a man who played tennis before breakfast even though he was apt to work on his libretti until 3 a.m.; who endured gout and headaches, and in the evening gambled mildly at West End clubs: 'Good dinner. Rainy night. Row with cabman – refused to take us – made him – paid him bare fare – abusive – gave him card – number 8630 . . . played penny bank – lost £2. Left at 12.30.' The diary shows that at the Beefsteak Club Henry Labouchère, Liberal MP and journalist, was one of his confrères: here and elsewhere (in some of the *Bab Ballads,* for instance) there are indications that W.S.G.'s political stance was probably more Liberal than Sullivan's Conservatism, though this changed later.

Gilbert's days were crowded with writing, business interviews, rehearsals, coaching his stars. He had taken under his wing Marion Terry, the twenty-six-year-old actress sister of Ellen Terry. She is 'M.T.' in the diary and 'Mrs' is his wife. Marion lived with them at The Boltons for periods and accompanied them on holidays. Occasionally Gilbert's old father William came to stay. On one diary page we have a pen-picture of W.S.G. reading *David Copperfield* aloud to the family circle, including 'M.T.' On another we find W.S.G. and 'Mrs' taking a jaunt to Dieppe where he has an early morning dip at one end of the beach – 'Mrs apart', in accordance with bathing etiquette. Nothing of private life is allowed to appear in the diary, but when he visits Portsmouth with Sullivan to gather nautical background for their next opera the description becomes quite expansive. They go aboard H.M.S. *Thunderer*: 'Lunched on board – went round ship – then Lord C. Beresford told off boatman and four men to take us on board various ships – went to *Invincible, Victory* and *St Vincent*, making sketches on last two – then pulled ashore to station.'

Back home at The Boltons, Gilbert had a toy theatre: in it he constructed a half-inch scale model of a warship's quarter-deck, with coloured blocks

Marion Terry, Gilbert's protégée and an actress whose talents rivalled her more famous sister's. She often stayed with the Gilberts for long periods and went on holidays with them to Margate.

'Mr Peters takes a bath at Boulogne', a sketch made by Gilbert after a holiday in France with 'Mrs'.

View of Portsmouth Harbour in
1881; Nelson's flagship, the *Victory*,
can be seen in the centre.

of wood representing the characters. With the aid of this theatre, and of
sketches and diagrams in his plot-books, he always went to first rehearsals
thoroughly prepared. He was especially punctilious over details in the case
of this burlesque of naval occasions, *H.M.S. Pinafore*, for as a boy he had
been introduced to the sea by his father, the naval surgeon, and he felt the
salty blood of his imagined ancestor Sir Humphrey racing in his veins. He
even had the uniforms for *Pinafore* made by a Portsmouth naval tailor.
Everything must be shipshape, no matter how farcical a plot in which the
First Lord of the Admiralty is piped aboard the *Pinafore* accompanied by

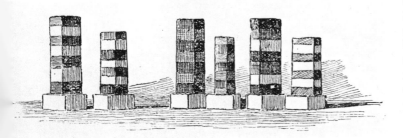

Sketches made by Gilbert for *H.M.S. Pinafore* during his visit to Portsmouth. (*Left*) Gilbert's characters': blocks representing male members of the cast were three inches high, those for female members half an inch shorter; different colours denoted the different voices. With the blocks Gilbert would work out every detail of his stage productions in advance.

W. H. Smith, Disraeli's First Lord of the Admiralty.

an admiring bevy of 'his cousins, his sisters, and his aunts'. Gilbert was nervous lest his First Lord be thought a caricature of the real First Lord in Disraeli's government, W. H. Smith, founder of the newsagent firm. This uncharacteristic qualm was perhaps in deference to Sullivan's high-flown Tory friends, for in a letter to 'Dear S.' Gilbert assures him that 'of course there will be no personality in this – the fact that the First Lord in the opera is a radical of the most pronounced type will do away with any suspicion that W. H. Smith is intended.' The Gilbertian First Lord was indeed radically risen from the lower orders, having ascended to the Cabinet by observing the maxim 'Stick close to your desks and never go to sea, And you all may be Rulers of the Queen's Navee!' Nevertheless the comparison was so inevitable that Disraeli was soon to dub his Minister 'Pinafore Smith'.

Following a fair success with *The Sorcerer* in London and on tour, the partnership needed a world-wide winner to achieve their enduring primacy and in *Pinafore* it came, but only after weathering perilous storms. Gilbert's first ideas for the plot reached Sullivan when he was at Nice, gambling excessively and enduring the first agonies of what was to be a lifelong bladder illness. In no mood for work, he rejected an invitation from the Leeds Musical Festival to compose an oratorio. Riviera sunshine and a promise of a hundred guineas from Leeds changed his mind and he returned to London searching for a subject not already touched by Mendelssohn or Handel. This was all swept aside by the flurry of preparations for *H.M.S. Pinafore*: 'I would compose a few bars and then be almost insensible from pain. When the paroxysm was passed I would write a little more, until the pain over-whelmed me again. Never was music written under such distressing conditions.' Yet on 25 May 1878 he conducted the first performance with radiant enthusiasm.

First nights were always Gilbert's nightmare. A worried author-producer perambulated the streets. On that of *H.M.S. Pinafore*: 'Went in and out three or four times during evening. Enthusiastic calls for self and Sullivan. Then to Beefsteak.' First editions of the newspapers were scanned with anxiety, turning to joy: all approved, except the *Daily Telegraph*, which pronounced it 'a frothy production destined soon to subside into nothingness.' Within a few days it looked as though the *Telegraph* was right. The most apparent cause was a May heat-wave; then, during a blazing June, *Pinafore* was almost stifled to death. Sullivan was at the Paris Exhibition arranging and conducting concerts of English music. When he returned to sweltering London, adorned with the ribbon of the Légion d'Honneur, he found receipts at the Opéra Comique down to £40 and less.

According to Jessie Bond, one of the principals, a mean theatre in a slummy area where audiences 'perspired and gasped' was 'not quite the place for decent and respectable people'. But some who saw *H.M.S. Pinafore* were affronted for another reason. They could not stomach Gilbert's satire upon Things British. Mr Disraeli – now Lord Beaconsfield – wrote that except at Wycombe Fair in his youth he had 'never seen anything so bad as *Pinafore*'. It was not only Gilbert's mockery of the system of appointing non-technical civilians to the head of highly technical Services (e.g. W. H. Smith); he actually dared to poke fun at class distinction in the Senior Service, where

Two illustrations by Gilbert to his *Pinafore* songs: (*left*) 'For in spite of all temptations To belong to other nations, He remains an Englishman!' and (*right*) 'A British tar is a soaring soul'.

superiority of rank was solely due to 'an accident of birth', as the First Lord, Sir Joseph Porter, declares. To give the satire a double twist Sir Joseph is presented as an upstart snob making a show of his enlightened democracy.

For one cause and another it looked as though this opera must be written off. Carte, Sullivan and Gilbert had faith in its quality: they only wished to weather the heat-wave. So did the cast, who voluntarily cut a third of their salaries; but the directors of the Comedy Opera Company wished to cut their losses. Six times they put up notices dismissing the cast, only to be countermanded by Carte. If *H.M.S. Pinafore* had been shipwrecked, the indications are that Sullivan and Gilbert would have been sufficiently discouraged to give up further collaboration in comic opera. Gilbert's diary shows that his mind was running again towards serious drama. Sullivan's thoughts were turning to Leeds. Although the partners now seemed to be in danger of splitting apart in one direction, they came together most un-expectedly in another, a sacred musical drama entitled *The Martyr of Antioch*, adapted by Mr Gilbert. This project was a far cry from their popular alliance. Moreover, on returning from a summer holiday in Switzerland Sullivan wrote a stiff note to 'My dear Carte' complaining that he had called at the theatre and 'found the Orchestra both in number and efficiency very different to what it was when I rehearsed the *Pinafore*.' Unless the deficiencies were met by engaging better players he would withdraw his music im-mediately. 'You know perfectly well that what I say I mean. Kindly advise the Directors of this.' Mediocrity of performance was not Sullivan's idea of rescuing *Pinafore*. But the slump was a hard fact.

It was a convenient chance that Sullivan conducted the Promenade Concerts at Covent Garden that year, with an eclectic choice of items ranging from Beethoven's Choral Symphony to a selection from *Pinafore*. The latter was such a tremendous success that Sullivan played it again. People started talking about the opera. By the end of August the theatre was full at every performance. D'Oyly Carte was organizing touring companies. Music shops sold ten thousand copies of the piano score in one day. PINAFORE MANIA!, shouted the headlines. Carte rewarded the actors and actresses at the Opéra Comique by organizing a picnic on the Thames to Windsor, thus founding what was to be an annual outing.

H.M.S. Pinafore: Gilbert and Sullivan's ship comes home. (*Left*) Jessie Bond as Hebe and George Grossmith as Sir Joseph Porter in the first production; (*above*) Captain Corcoran in embryo: Gilbert's early *Bab Ballad* character, Captain Reece. (*Below*) A letter from W.S.G. indicating his proposed set design and (*right*) a contemporary artist's impression of a scene from Act Two of the opera.

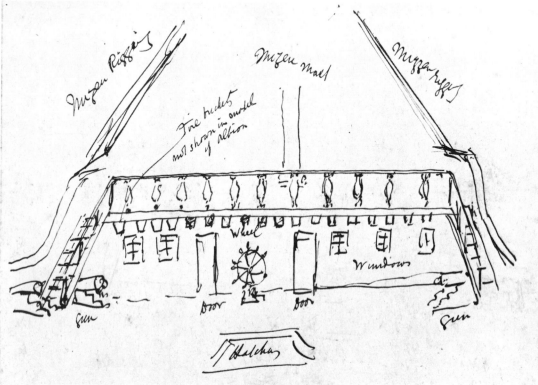

June 8, 1878.

55

Now it was prosperity all round. Gilbert bought himself a seagoing yacht, the *Druidess*, and had an adventure when he and 'Mrs' made their first voyage in her from the Isle of Wight to Ramsgate. They ran into heavy weather at night and had difficulty in making Dungeness for shelter and safety. Gilbert's diary records that after this experience he took lessons in navigation!

Since an unauthorized production of *Trial by Jury* in New York in 1875 the works of Gilbert and Sullivan had been pirated in the United States, and not a dollar came back. As no international copyright then existed, American theatre managements considered themselves within their legal rights in presenting the operas without permission and without payment to the British authors. Now, in 1878, came news that the *Pinafore* mania was sweeping the States. Five theatres in New York were playing highly Americanized *Pinafores*; all were packed. 'Such a furore as this opera has created I have never known before in the history of the American stage,' wrote a journalist in the Land of the Free. Across the States scores of managements rushed to join this free gold-rush. Sullivan received a cable offering him £1,000 to conduct the opera in Philadelphia for a fortnight; he had to refuse because (as he wrote to Hollingshead) 'I have been suffering martyrdom for a fortnight.' He had an operation which he believed to be to crush a stone in the kidney. Modern urological opinion is that it was almost certainly in the bladder. Wherever it was, a stone was then extremely difficult to deal with; for one thing, there were no X-rays to locate it. Whatever the doctors did, Sullivan had to convalesce in the Engadine. Meanwhile Carte departed to the United States to see what could be done to combat the copyright pirates. In his absence came piracy in London by, of all people, Carte's fellow directors, Water-cart Bailey and Co. These financiers no longer wished to suspend *Pinafore* (they had invested £500 each, and were now drawing £500 a week). They made the extraordinary decision to split from Carte and open their own separate production of the opera at the Aquarium Theatre, and they sent horse-vans and an army of thugs to the Opéra Comique with the intention of taking away the scenery. They did not even wait until the end of the performance and a free fight broke out behind the scenes. The curtain was lowered while the First Lord of the Admiralty reassured the bewildered audience. All boarders were repelled. Bailey and Co., whose rival production survived only 91 performances, were taken to court by Carte-Sullivan-Gilbert. Litigation dragged on for over a year. At length (said Carte), 'We won the case of course but in the meantime the Company had gone bankrupt, we got no damages and had to pay our own costs.' The consequence was an historic agreement drawn up in Gilbert's handwriting: a partnership signed by him-self, Sullivan and Carte, each putting up £1,000 capital: 'The profits of the speculation to be equally divided after all expenses have been paid. Carte's salary to be £15 per week – Sullivan's and Gilbert's fees to be four guineas per representation, each. These salaries and pay to be included in weekly expenses.' This was the simple basis for a long partnership. Though amended by subsequent agreements it established the equal sharing of profits 'after all expenses have been paid' – a phrase which was to cause trouble at the time of the 'Carpet Quarrel' twelve years later.

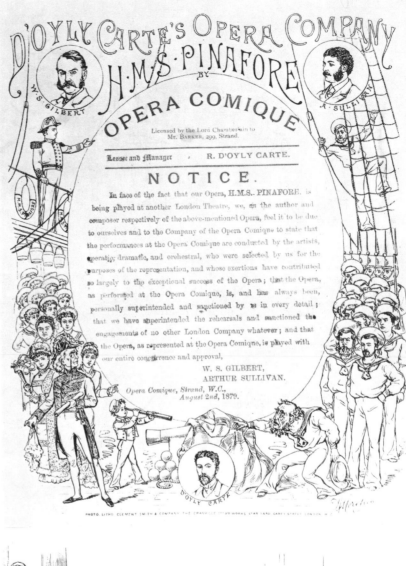

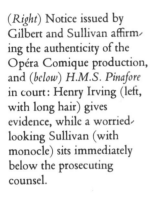

(*Right*) Notice issued by Gilbert and Sullivan affirming the authenticity of the Opéra Comique production, and (*below*) *H.M.S. Pinafore* in court: Henry Irving (left, with long hair) gives evidence, while a worried-looking Sullivan (with monocle) sits immediately below the prosecuting counsel.

Helen Lenoir, the remarkable ex-actress and businesswoman who became Carte's secretary and later his wife. The daughter of William Cowper Black, procurator fiscal of Wigtownshire in Scotland, she spoke several languages and, besides shouldering many of the burdens of mounting the Gilbert and Sullivan operas during her husband's life, ran the D'Oyly Carte Company for eight years after his death.

Meanwhile Carte's reconnoitre in America had shown that the pirates were making fortunes from *Pinafores* of infinite variety: one interpolated a song about a new fashion in trousers, another managed to work in the 'Hallelujah Chorus'. Characters were interpreted with un-Gilbertian freedom, as when Little Buttercup was played by a man seven feet tall 'with all the dainty coyness of a woman', it was alleged. One or two productions out of perhaps a hundred and fifty in the States had some merit, and the *American Register* made the remarkable prophecy that 'this comparatively unimportant work may be the means of starting the regeneration of the modern stage in our native land'.

Carte reported that many American singers had excellent voices but 'not the remotest idea of how to play the piece. The acting, costumes, time of music, etc. are too atrociously bad for words to express.' If the creators of the opera were to retrieve anything from America they had to confront not only pirates but incompetent pirates; therefore Carte proposed that the best plan was for Sullivan and Gilbert to get across the Atlantic quickly and give New York an eyeful of the authentic *Pinafore*, followed by 'our new trump card the New Opera' – as yet unnamed, but already being written. They must carry the fight into the pirates' camp.

Carte returned to London with 'splendid terms' signed by American managements. He told Sullivan that *Pinafore* tunes were heard everywhere.

'A hundred thousand barrel-organs were constructed to play nothing else,' joked Sullivan; but his real feeling about the misuse of his music is shown in his reaction to a letter he received from Helen Lenoir, Carte's secretary (later his second wife), advising him that the proprietor of the South London Palace had asked permission to use a Sullivan song there: 'As I don't know whether you like any "*Pinafore*" songs sung at *Music Halls*, I should be much obliged if you would kindly advise me as to your wishes.' The South London, a short distance from Sullivan's humble birthplace in Lambeth, was one of those gin-and-joke palaces, half-pub, half-theatre, where the customers sat drinking while the chairman introduced with stentorian voice the buxom charmers and rough-and-tumble comics of Victorian vaudeville. Sullivan scribbled two words across the letter: 'Certainly not.'

Legitimate use of Gilbert and Sullivan works in Britain was another thing. Carte introduced the system of licensing amateur societies, a connection which has no equal in theatre history and has done a great deal to strengthen the hold of these operas on the British public. The first amateur performance in Britain was *H.M.S. Pinafore* at the Drill Hall, Kingston-on-Thames, on 30 April 1879, by the Harmonists' Choral Society.

The professional *Pinafore* was doing wonderful business: 571 performances in London, and two touring companies reaching every town of any size. Gilbert accordingly bought a bigger and better yacht, *Pleione*, and during the summer of 1879 went sailing along the south coast of England, ruminating on the plot of the next opera, *The Pirates of Penzance*. Carte insisted that it must be ready as an immediate successor to *H.M.S. Pinafore* in Britain and as a master-stroke to beat the American pirates: a first night in New York was his device to this end. They sought to keep Sullivan to a time-table – which was far from easy, for he still had lapses of sickness, he was temperamentally an eleventh-hour worker, and *The Martyr of Antioch* hung round his neck. This was promised for the next Leeds Festival, and Sullivan was 'very seriously perplexed how to manage it', he wrote to the Festival Committee. Gilbert had started writing *The Pirates*. Lyrics in his spidery handwriting were winged two miles across London by the Post Office, which in Queen Victoria's bountiful days delivered ten times daily in Westminster. There Sullivan was sketching the music and if difficulty arose with the words they were posted back to Gilbert who went to great trouble over revisions.

Sullivan and Gilbert seldom met socially. One rare conviviality was in 1879 when they met at the Garrick, Sullivan's club; they discussed *The Pirates*, then were joined by the Duke of Edinburgh. After dinner they all drove to Sullivan's place where others gathered and Mrs Ronalds sang, and after she had departed the men played cribbage until Gilbert had lost £3 and decided at 3 a.m. that it was time to go home to Kitty.

By August he told Carte: 'I've broken the back of Act Two and see my way clearly to the end. I think it comes out very well.' Carte booked the Fifth Avenue Theatre, New York. The première of a British opera in America! It would be unprecedented. Moreover, if they kept words and music strictly in manuscript (no printing) it should foil the pirates. Secrecy was therefore essential in the anti-pirate campaign. On 5 November Gilbert and Sullivan approached New York aboard the liner *Bothnia*; in their bags

The Fifth Avenue Theatre, New York, shortly after its opening in 1873.

was the still unfinished text and music of *The Pirates*. Their plan was first to produce their authentic British version of *H.M.S. Pinafore* for a short run. They were given an impudent reception off Sandy Hook by a fleet of steamers manned by pirates, no less: 'Every vessel in the motley squadron', reported the *Musical Times*, 'was dressed with American and English flags, and having on board a *Pinafore* band and chorus. The Standard *Pinafore* sent two tugs, and the Church Choir *Pinafore* one; another hailing from the Aquarium, another from Chickering Hall, another from Lexington Avenue, and another from some place where a German version of the operetta is played.' But the effect was spoiled by a 'pestilent little tug' sent out by a rival entertainment – The Nigger Minstrels – carrying a flag with the terrible legend NO PINAFORE!, and blasting its hooter to drown the cacophony of tunes from the opera.

All this upset Gilbert's digestion, and Sullivan was angered when he read in the *New York Herald* that 'The Lost Chord' and other ballads were 'echoing in a thousand drawing-rooms' (no royalties to the composer); but the partners preserved good British equanimity when interviewed by reporters. The *New York Herald* remarked that, contrary to reputation, 'Two more amiable, modest, simple, good humored and vivacious men could not easily be imagined. They fairly brim over with animation, high spirits and the jolliest kind of bonhomie.' The reporter added that Mr Gilbert was expected to drop a witticism every time he opened his mouth. This was true, and at times the adoration of the Americans provoked him beyond equanimity. At one New York reception a gushing lady said 'Dear Mr Gilbert, your friend Sullivan's music is *too* delightful. It reminds me so much of dear *Baytch*. Do tell me what is *Baytch* doing just now. Is he still composing?' 'No, madam. Just now dear Bach is by way of decomposing.'

The first night of the authentic *Pinafore* at the Fifth Avenue on 1 December 1879 was a revelation to the Americans, who now saw the author's polished production and heard Sullivan's genuine orchestrations for the first time. He wrote to his mother: 'At last I really think I shall get a little money out of America. I ought to, for they have made a good deal out of me. . . . In order to strike while the iron is hot, and get all the profit we can while everyone is talking about it, we are sending out three companies to other towns in America, and all these have to be selected, organized, and rehearsed.'

Simultaneously *The Pirates of Penzance* was being prepared for its première at the Fifth Avenue Theatre on New Year's Eve. No details were given to the press except Gilbert's remark that 'the treatment will be similar to that of *Pinafore*, namely to treat a thoroughly farcical subject in a thoroughly serious manner'. Someone has said that *The Pirates* is *H.M.S. Pinafore* transferred to dry land. Instead of satire on the navy there is satire on the army, the police, and the Englishman's sense of duty (*The Slave of Duty* is the opera's sub-title). Instead of a landlubbing First Lord of the Admiralty we have a Major-General whose military knowledge, though he is 'plucky and adventury, has only been brought down to the beginning of the century'.

Suddenly, with less than a fortnight to go before the first night, Sullivan made an appalling discovery; he had left all his musical sketches for Act One in London. No ship was speedy enough to recover them. Rehearsals of Act Two were in full swing while Sullivan tackled the stupendous task of rewriting, and now he was stricken again by his illness. He was in tortures of pain as he dragged himself from his couch, writing all day and far into the night. He finished the full score of *The Pirates of Penzance* at 7 a.m. on 28 December. Next day came full dress rehearsals: 'In despair because it went so badly.' He composed the Overture (helped by his friend Alfred Cellier) and rehearsed it with the ink hardly dry on the band-parts. On New Year's Eve, before 'one of the most fashionable audiences of the season' (*New York Herald*), he entered the orchestra, in his own words 'more dead than alive, but got better when I took the stick in my hand. Fine reception. Piece went marvellously well.' Celebrations kept him from his bed until 7 a.m.: 'Felt utterly worn out.'

During the performance the American plagiarists had attempted to take shorthand notes in the theatre and they offered bribes, in vain, to members of the orchestra for the band-parts. After every performance all music was

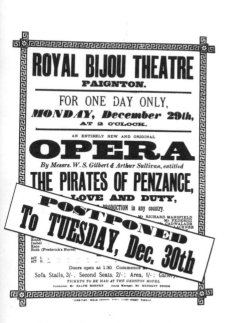

(*Above*) Poster advertising the Paignton 'copyrighting' première of *The Pirates of Penzance* on 30 December 1879. Paignton was chosen simply because D'Oyly Carte's touring company happened to be playing *Pinafore* in the area at the time. (*Right*) The programme for the first London production in 1880.

locked in a safe, and no printed copies of *The Pirates* were on sale in the theatre, as had been customary in England. All this foiled the piratical tycoons, if only for a time. A few hours before the New York première a copyrighting performance was given in England: at two o'clock in the afternoon of 30 December the curtain rose upon one of the most bizarre shows ever put on any stage, at the tiny Royal Bijou Theatre at Paignton. In that quiet resort on the south Devon coast only some fifty people turned out for the performance. Only scraps of the music had arrived from New York. The pirates were denoted by having handkerchiefs tied round their heads, and the chorus of policemen marched on dressed as sailors. Instead of bull's-eye lanterns they carried scripts which they had not had time to learn.

Gilbert had sent an early draft of the script to Helen Lenoir, who supervised the Paignton performance. A comparison between it and the text used in America and later in London shows intriguing differences; one of them again illustrates W.S.G.'s democratic leanings. In the Paignton version a satirical thrust at Britain's hereditary peerage was delivered by the Major-General:

> Let foreigners look down with scorn
> On legislators heaven-born;
> We know what limpid wisdom runs
> From Peers and all their eldest Sons.
> Enrapt the true-born Briton hears
> The wisdom of his House of Peers.

In New York the author struck this out in favour of the famous declaration (used now) that 'with all our faults, we love our House of Peers.'

Sullivan's opinion of *The Pirates* is important as showing his accord with Gilbert at this point in their partnership. He wrote to Mum: 'The libretto is ingenious, clever, wonderfully funny in parts, and sometimes brilliant in dialogue – beautifully written for music, as is all Gilbert does, and all the action and business perfect. The music is infinitely superior in every way to the *Pinafore* – tunier, and more developed – of a higher class altogether.' And another tribute to Gilbert: Sullivan had never seen 'such a beautiful combination of colour and form on any stage . . . the girls look as if they had stepped bodily out of the frame of a Gainsborough picture. The New York ladies are raving about them.'

This invasion of the USA by a purely British style of stage show took place long before the American nation had evolved its modern idiom of popular music through the commercialization of Negro folk-rhythms – blues and spirituals – into jazz, ragtime and swing. Nick('Tiger Rag') LaRocca was not born until 1889. Irving Berlin was born in 1888, George Gershwin not until ten years later. So Sullivan heard no jazz in 1880. His diary shows that he found New York society rather like that of a quiet English provincial city, and there was a great regard for anything from London; it is not so surprising that America should fall for so *English* an entertainment as Gilbert and Sullivan opera.

The USA in 1880 had less than fifty million inhabitants, only fifteen million more than Great Britain. The pioneers were still opening up the Golden West. Hollywood was a place where they grew lemons. Mr F.W. Woolworth had just started his five- and ten-cent stores. Alexander Graham Bell had invented the telephone four years before and Thomas Edison had invented the talking machine a year later. Into this exciting new land Dr Sullivan and Mr Gilbert now plunged, pioneers themselves, travelling up and down the States.

Everywhere they were lionized. Everywhere theatres were packed by their productions. This marked the opening of an epoch: a flow of English entertainment was established westwards across the Atlantic, rather than in the reverse direction.

Gilbert enjoyed travelling the States less than Sullivan, who adored the 'affectionate nature' (he said) of American ladies, and whose social round took him into Canada to stay with the Governor-General. He was delighted when asked to conduct concerts of his serious music, especially *The Prodigal*

Marion Hood as Mabel wearing one of the ravishing costumes designed for the London production of *The Pirates*.

View of Broadway, New York, in 1882.

Son by the highly esteemed Handel and Haydn Society of Boston. It was reported that he and Gilbert received $4,000 (£830) a week during the first six weeks of their authentic *Pirates* in New York alone. But their triumph did not spell entire defeat for the piratical managements, who managed in time to get hold of Sullivan's orchestral score; one of their lawyers even argued that the copyrighting performance at Paignton had actually made *The Pirates* anyone's property in the USA! From now onwards, for years, Carte instructed his lawyers to pursue the pirates from state to state, applying for injunctions. Some cases were won, others lost, but the over-all impact on American public opinion of the true Gilbertian productions was that their superiority over spurious imitators was recognized. It was the same in Australia: a confusing legal position was beaten by authentic productions licensed by Carte, from *H.M.S. Pinafore* onwards.

Net receipts (earned by my profession)
from 1st January 1880 to 31st December 1880

	£.	s.	d.
Metzler & Co. Royalties.			
Christmas '79. £900. Midsum '80 - 824.15			
	1724	15	-
Boosey & Co. ditto.			
373 - 11 - 3. and 304 - 12 - 11 =	678	4	2
America - Pirates of Penzance. (net)	2637	9	
Opera Comique. Pinafore.	655	4	
Ditto. Pirate of Penzance.	2517	11	
ditto - Bal: of Pinafore & Children.	100	16	
Country night of pieces - half paid Xmas.	725	0	
Australian ditto	150	-	
India ditto. & Co, & Box.	41		
School of Music - 2 terms.	266	13	4
Tennyson Song. (Kegan Paul & Co)	42	0	0
Leeds Festival	315	-	
Australian night - Pinafore. 2nd year.	135	-	

£. 9988 - 12 - 6

When they returned to England from America in March 1880 Gilbert (aged forty-three) and Sullivan (thirty-seven) had won international fame and princely fortune. On the London first night of *The Pirates of Penzance*, 3 April 1880, it was notable that music (as distinct from theatre) critics were now present in force. One of them, in the *Musical World*, remarked on Sullivan's 'masterly skill in instrumentation' and his 'power of making his instruments almost laugh with his text'. Comic opera was becoming respectable. None the less, Sullivan was looking forward to the fruits of a letter he had received from the redoubtable Fred Spark, editor of the *Leeds Express* and Secretary of the Leeds Triennial Musical Festivals. Previous festivals had been directed by Sir Michael Costa, the fashionable Italian-born composer, but his imperious manner had alienated the tough Yorkshiremen. Difficulties had also arisen between the Leeds Committee and their next

Punch's view of Sullivan in 1880.

choice, Charles Hallé, the German-born founder of the Hallé Orchestra ('Your Manchester band is not sufficiently good for a Leeds Festival,' wrote Spark). Now Leeds offered Sullivan two hundred guineas to conduct the entire Festival in October 1880, in addition to the hundred guineas already agreed for composing *The Martyr of Antioch*.

When Sullivan visited Leeds to meet the Committee in June he told them they had conferred upon him 'almost the greatest honour that could be held by any man'; he asked them to augment the orchestra to a hundred and twenty players; and he got the Duke of Edinburgh to be President of the Festival.

The large choir recruited from towns in the West Riding of Yorkshire was proud of itself and of its new director. Sullivan made it greater through his sensitive handling of classical works. He was popular with chorus, orchestra, artists, and audience. His first Leeds Festival beat all records of attendance (14,854) and profit (£2,371). His own *Martyr of Antioch* had a lukewarm reception from the music critics, but not from Gilbert: 'Of the many substantial advantages that have resulted to me from our association this last is and always will be the most highly prized,' he assured Sullivan, and for once there was no financial advantage, Gilbert having declined payment for his adaptation. Although he had not heard the performance he added that he supposed it would 'endure until music itself shall die'. His absence from Leeds was ostensibly due to his alleged lack of appreciation of serious music; actually he was up to his neck in the exceptionally troublesome task of writing the next comic opera, to succeed *The Pirates of Penzance*, now running towards its 363rd performance at the Opéra Comique.

Patience was hard to create, firstly because Gilbert initially wrote two-thirds of a comedy on the rivalry of a couple of curates for their infatuated lady parishioners but then abandoned it ('I distrust the clerical element,' he remarked); secondly because he then switched to a theme that was difficult, but which afforded opportunities for social satire unsurpassed in the whole Gilbert and Sullivan canon: aestheticism. In 1880 London's fashionable salons were full of languid ladies and affected men. The movement towards beauty in daily life which had been led so healthily by William Morris, Edward Burne-Jones, Dante Gabriel Rossetti and James McNeill Whistler had now swung to extremes of 'aesthetic' fashions and medieval posturing, all ridiculously mixed up with a vogue for Japanese fans and jars which had turned upper-middle-class England into something like an Oriental bazaar. The sardonic eye of Mr Gilbert observed that to be an apostle of the high aesthetic band you had only to 'Walk down Piccadilly with a poppy or a lily in your medieval hand'. He transferred his lovesick maidens' infatuation to Bunthorne, 'a fleshly poet' not far removed from Oscar Wilde (who was just publishing his first slim volume of poems), though Bunthorne is not a direct caricature: the Gilbertian jibe was at cults. Gilbert himself designed the costumes; Carte bought the fabrics at Liberty's, who specialized in aesthetic draperies and beads and potteries; the décor and attitudinizing of the characters was a skit on Pre-Raphaelite art and the melancholy attitudes of a Burne-Jones painting. For some time the aesthetes of art and literature had been lampooned in *Punch*, notably by George du Maurier's cartoons; now the satire was transferred to the stage with fresh Gilbertian adroitness.

Painters and art critics had recently been shaken by a bitter controversy, culminating in a libel case, and this gave the subject a topicality which Gilbert was quick to seize upon. Whistler had sued Ruskin, supreme art critic of the day, for writing that Whistler with his paintings called *Nocturnes* at the Grosvenor Gallery was flinging a pot of paint in the public's face. Gilbert's diary reveals that W.S.G. took the keenest interest in the proceedings. On the morning of the first day of the trial he took breakfast with Whistler. The 'greenery-yallery, Grosvenor Gallery, foot-in-the-grave young man' of *Patience*, however, is not Whistler but a type of phoney art-flirter. Gilbert and D'Oyly Carte, both friendly with Whistler, were not men to knock his art. Carte put *Patience*'s aim in a publicity circular: the new art movements, he said, had rendered 'our everyday existence more pleasant and more beautiful' but latterly had 'given place to the outpourings of a clique of professors of ultra-refinement who preach the gospel of morbid languor and sickly sensuousness, which is half real and half affected by its high priests for the purpose of gaining social notoriety. The authors of *Patience* have not desired to cast ridicule on the true aesthetic spirit, but only to attack the unmanly oddities which masquerade in its likeness.'

Patience: the follies of an age caricatured.
(*Above*) Embroidered panels by William
Morris from the Red House, illustrating the
contemporary passion for things medieval
and (*right*) the three dragoons aping aesthetic
postures in the original production of *Patience*.

(*Left*) Cartoon by George du Maurier from *Punch*: du Maurier's character Jellaby Postlethwaite epitomized the aesthetic movement for many Victorians. (*Below*) A modern production of the opera by the Sadler's Wells Opera Company, London.

Oscar Wilde, complete with lily, lecturing in America.

It is a phenomenon in English social history that only ten years after Gilbert and Sullivan had begun their partnership with *Thespis*, they dared to go before the public with an almost highbrow comedy of manners; *Patience* is a mark of the revolution in public taste. Its target was affectation, as duty is that of *The Pirates* and discipline that of *H.M.S. Pinafore*. Gilbert feared that 'aestheticism' was a passing phase, and that *Patience* would pass with it. He need not have worried. This opera still appeals to the public, not only for its incidental wit and music, but because its basic subject is always with us. We still have our *poseurs* of art and fashion, our 'miminy, piminy, *je-ne-sais-quoi* young men'. They are not unknown on television.

Patience marks a command over theatrical effect which Sullivan and Gilbert had not hitherto achieved. After opening the opera in pastel shades, matched by music of a similarly mellow quality, it is a *coup de théâtre* to bring on the scarlet Dragoon Guards to a strapping, virile chorus. The entire atmosphere is transformed in a moment. The 35th Heavy Dragoons, in contrast to the aesthetes, are tough, unimaginative military men, conquerors of the world. Here again Gilbert holds up his satirical mirror to life. The 1880s were a period when the British were bent on colonial conquest. They had just fought the Zulus (Gilbert had been invited by *The Times* to go as war correspondent, his diary reveals). From Egypt to Fiji the redcoats were making their presence felt. Those plumed helmets and scarlet uniforms were

70

designed to scare the fuzzy-wuzzies abroad, and flutter the hearts of the women at home. The military music came as second nature to one bred in the world of Sandhurst, but Sullivan's efforts to deliver music in time for Gilbert's rehearsals were retarded by long spells at Nice: 'Occasionally I try to find a new idea . . . but my natural indolence, aided by the sunshine, prevents my doing any really serious work.' Nevertheless the *Patience* score is of no mean order, rich in its lucidity to underline and to strengthen the various characters and the action. Back in London, the light in Sullivan's music-room burned nightly until quenched by the light of day, right up to the première on 23 April 1881 at the Opéra Comique.

Oscar Wilde himself was in the stalls. 'There with the sacred daffodil', reported the *Sporting Times*, 'stood the exponent of uncut hair.' This newspaper had printed a rumour that Richard D'Oyly Carte intended to send Wilde to America 'as a sandwich man for *Patience*'. It was half true. Carte, still running his lecture agency, had booked Wilde for an American tour, and he wrote to Helen Lenoir, who was in New York managing his interests there: 'Wilde is slightly sensitive, although I don't think appallingly so; . . . I told him he must not mind my using a little bunkum to push him in America. You must deal with it when he arrives.' Accordingly, Wilde turned up at *Patience* at the Standard Theatre, New York, and was suitably recognized, to the benefit of both opera and lecture tour.

There were no flies on showman Carte. He had a far more historic *tour de force* in preparation. In London a bigger and better theatre was being built between the Strand and the Embankment, with seats for 1,292 persons and, sensationally, electric light – 'the first time it has been attempted to light any public building entirely by electricity', boasted Carte in a hand-out as interesting for what it reveals of the man as of his Savoy Theatre: 'The greatest drawbacks to the enjoyment of the theatrical performances are, undoubtedly, the foul air and heat which pervade all theatres. As everyone knows, each gas-burner consumes as much oxygen as many people, and causes great heat besides. The incandescent lamps consume *no* oxygen, and cause no perceptible heat.' Determined to go the whole hog with his reforms, he also announced the abolition of that source of annoyance to the public – tipping: 'The attendants will be paid fair wages.' Programmes were also free.

Patience was transferred to the new theatre on 10 October 1881 with 'entirely new scenery, dresses and increased chorus', to suit brighter lighting and a larger stage. The High Society audience that night included the Prince of Wales, a battery of barons, Mrs Ronalds glowing with her personal electricity, and Oscar Wilde again. Everyone was delighted by the elegance of an auditorium in cream and gold, with proscenium curtains in rich yellow satin embroidered in the Spanish style, all fit to turn the head of any aesthete: 'Nothing so tenderly loving in colour and design has ever yet been seen in London,' said one. Fingers pointed to the electric bulbs and it was assumed that their *not* being lit, as the auxiliary gas-lamps were, indicated a coming touch of showmanship by 'Dear D'Oyly'. With a panache suited to such a signal occasion, the curtains parted to reveal the entire company singing 'God Save the Queen', all three verses arranged and conducted by Sullivan to have a dramatic cumulative effect, starting with sopranos and rising to a grand

Interior of the Savoy Theatre during the opening run of *Patience*, showing the revolutionary electric lighting which is also seen (*right*) as a decorative motif incorporated in the programme for the opera.

tutti. With all this came a disappointment. Dear D'Oyly stepped forward to beg the indulgence of his public: lighting twelve hundred electric lamps was unprecedented, all at once, and the contractors had found that the 120-horsepower steam-engine placed on an adjoining vacant plot to drive a generator did not supply sufficient electricity. Another engine would be installed; meanwhile the stage must remain gas-lit, but the auditorium could be electrically lit at once. With a feeling of curiosity as to 'whether the electricity would work', reported the *Daily Chronicle*, the audience watched Carte sign for the gaslight to be lowered and then, 'As if by the wave of a fairy's wand the theatre immediately became filled with a soft, soothing light, clearer and far more grateful than gas.' The audience gave an astonished cheer. Eleven weeks later electricity was in full use not only on stage but backstage as well.

While Carte, the hero of the hour, was bathed in his electricity, Gilbert was offstage; for six months he had been at The Boltons, quietly working. Only nine days after the première of *Patience* Sullivan had jotted in his diary:

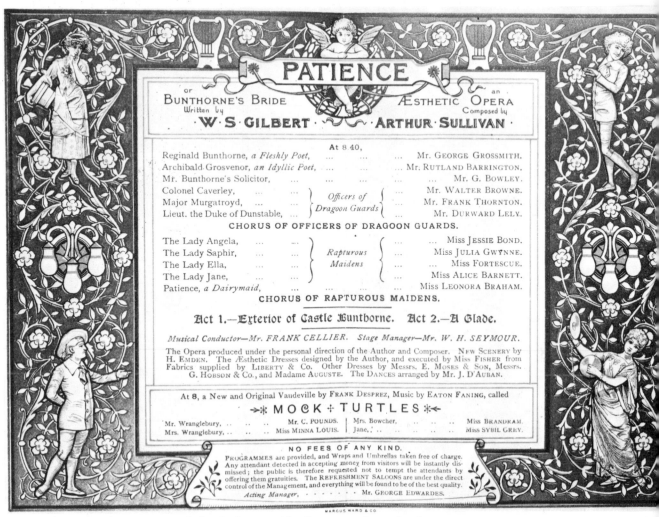

'Gilbert came this evening and sketched out an idea for a new piece – Lord Chancellor, Peers, Fairies, etc. Funny, but at present vague' – this was *Iolanthe*. Gilbert was a thruster, Sullivan a follower. He had too many other immediate interests to bother yet about their next comic opera. Off he went with the Duke of Edinburgh aboard H.M.S. *Hercules* to be entertained at Copenhagen by the King of Denmark, at St Petersburg by the Tsar of Russia, and at Kiel by the future Kaiser of First World War notoriety, who sang 'He polished up the handle of the big front door' to him. Sullivan's comment: 'It was too funny.' Later that year Sullivan was in Egypt, trying to write down Egyptian folk-music for future use, and playing 'riotous games' with the future King George V. All the time *Patience* was amassing its 578 performances in London. All the time the cheques were coming in. Sullivan and Gilbert were each earning more than the Prime Minister, Mr Gladstone. Sullivan moved into an extravagant suite of rooms at Queen's Mansions, Victoria Street, not far from Westminster Abbey. Its décor was an Arabian nightmare: lamps from the romantic East, antique Egyptian screens, Persian

Queen's Mansions, Victoria Street, where Sullivan made his London home from 1881 until his death.

hangings, Oriental divans under the encircling palms. Victoriana gone mad. Gilbert was less romantic and more go-ahead in the large mansion being built for him in Harrington Gardens, Kensington; it had such unusual amenities as central heating, a bathroom on every floor, and a telephone (£20 a year). He arranged that another 'instrument' be installed at the side of the stage at the Savoy, so that Big Brother could talk to the stage manager or anyone else he chose.

About now the first crack appeared in the triumvirate of opera-makers. The Savoy Theatre was Carte's personal venture; he let it to the Sullivan-

Sullivan was addicted to Oriental décor, but this corner of his Queen's Mansions sitting-room displays a fondness for relatively conventional Victorian clutter. Despite this, a contemporary journalist professed himself struck by the impression of 'artistic calm and physical comfort' the composer's rooms conveyed.

Gilbert-Carte partnership for the presentation of the operas, and when he put the rent at £4,000 a year Gilbert made a caustic comment on the price and Carte was hurt: 'Money is not everything to me,' he wrote to Sullivan, with whom he was on close terms, 'and I feel more about this tone he has taken than I care to say.' Another potential disturbance lay in Sullivan's larger operatic desires: he wished to compose a grand opera for Covent Garden, and discussed the subject of Mary Stuart with Carte (not Gilbert). The academic Sullivan was also planning his next Leeds Festival. A second Sullivan symphony had been proposed, and ideas had been floating round in Sullivan's mind since hearing that native music in Egypt.

Fortunately for the high name of English wit in words and music, the sophisticated script of *Iolanthe* appealed to Sullivan immensely. The target this time was the Legislature: the Commons as serenaded by the sentry at Westminster who sings that when those dull MPs divide 'They've got to leave that brain outside, And vote just as their leaders tell 'em to'; and the Peers dominated by a robust Queen of the fairies and finally whisked away on wings of song, led by their 'very susceptible' Lord Chancellor. Here is gaiety galore, but Sullivan also wove into the score those delicate cadences which so wisely give us a breathing-space now and then from topsy-turvy Gilbertianism. In the Arcadian shepherd and his shepherdess, the love element, is much of the sweet and gentle side of Sullivan's own character, and the fairy element took Sullivan back to the first success of his youth, the fairy music for *The Tempest*. The spell caught W.S.G. himself, judging by the sprightly doodles in his plot-book. In this heavy leather-bound volume ideas are born, developed, amended: it records months and years of work in Gilbert's study. Teasing out a plot takes scores of pages, then he turns to a

Sketches for *Iolanthe* from Gilbert's plot-books.

clean page and rewrites it from beginning to end. The fairies, for instance, were originally to have infatuated the massed barristers of the Northern Assize Circuit; one day W.S.G. scrawled in the plot-book 'They *must* be peers.' The House of Lords was a subject of controversy then as now; Gilbert's sallies were perennial, as when his Lord Mountararat says, 'With a House of Peers composed exclusively of people of intellect, what's to become of the House of Commons?'

Sullivan spent the hot and lazy summer of 1882 at a country-house party in Cornwall. But his fellow guests saw little of him. Here was composed, among other numbers, the mock-heroic march of the peers 'Bow, bow, ye lower middle classes' – for which spectacle Gilbert ordered replica robes of the various Orders from Queen Victoria's court robe-maker. He was meticulous in a less happy direction. Suddenly he faced his partners with a demand for economy. He compared expenses at the Savoy with those previously at the Opéra Comique: 'The gas bill at the Savoy costs £10 a week more than at the Comique – and this with electric light!' he wrote to Carte. 'If we play for a year to an average of £120 nightly receipts, we make at the Opéra Comique £9,000 a year – and we lose at the Savoy £3,000 a year. You will see at once that this is simple ruination.' This squall blew itself out, however, as Carte planned to send to New York a pre-rehearsed company to open *Iolanthe* on the same day as the London première, and as Gilbert worked like a giant on both companies, cracking the whip without fear or favour.

Prime Minister Gladstone was among the luminous first-night audience for *Iolanthe*. It was an electrical occasion in every sense of the word. Gilbert, bent on making the most of the new wonder, employed 'self-lighting fairies with electricity stored somewhere about the small of their backs,' reported *The Theatre*. Another spectacle was the use of the (real) band of the Grenadier Guards to head the procession of Peers. (Both of these exhilarating touches were abandoned in later years by the D'Oyly Carte Company.) As Sullivan

The first production of *Iolanthe*. The Wagnerian Fairy Queen especially delighted sophisticates in the audience.

conducted the performance with his usual vivacity the audience little realized that he was almost penniless. That morning he had learned that his brokers had gone bankrupt. Most of his savings were lost. He and Gilbert were cheered at the end, but when he got home Sullivan confided to his diary that he felt 'very low'.

The cutting-edge of satire in *Iolanthe* was sharper at the first few performances than later; two original solos were removed after a few nights, and they were both 'social-conscience' songs. One was Dickens-like in Gilbert's compassion for the underdog in the Victorian slum, directing the attention of the aristocracy to the drunk and the thief: 'I might be as bad – As unlucky, rather – If I'd only had Fagin for a father.' The other song was about the snobbery of riches: a Mr de Belville earned little recognition as a brilliant poet, painter and inventor but when a distant cousin died and left de Belville a million he was at once elevated to the House of Peers as a 'universal genius'. These songs were denounced by drama critics as 'unsuitable' and 'jarring' in comic opera. Whether Gilbert and Sullivan, in cutting them, were actuated

by artistic or political unsuitability is uncertain; if the latter, Gilbert's radicalism was weakening.

With *Iolanthe* the Savoy boomed. Cables from America reported a wonderful reception. Mr Gilbert moved into his expensive new house. Dr Sullivan soon recovered his spirits and his bank balance. Yet he had begun to hear in the applause of Savoy audiences a mockery of his deepest aspirations. He had not composed a serious work since three years ago (*The Martyr of Antioch*); his last oratorio was ten years ago (*The Light of the World*). The grand opera was still unwritten. It had not escaped Sullivan's notice that the critic of *The Theatre* wrote of *Iolanthe*: 'All the fairy music is charming. Wagnerian extravagances are here and there lightly, not irreverently, caricatured. The parody of "Die alte Weise" (*Tristan and Isolde*, Act 3), played whilst Iolanthe is rising from her watery prison, struck me as being uncommonly clever, and so did the Rhine daughter and Walküre reminders in the last scene. . . . In every respect *Iolanthe* sustains Dr Sullivan's reputation as the most spontaneous, fertile, and scholarly composer of comic opera this country has ever produced.' Very flattering; but at the same time disturbing to Sullivan, for another critic, in the *Globe*, had called him 'a masterly musician, content for awhile to partially sacrifice himself rather than hinder the clear enunciation of the words. . . .' To Sullivan this was rubbing salt publicly into a private wound. He was getting tired of sacrificing himself to

78

The Gilberts' home in Harrington Gardens, Kensington: (*far left*) the exterior and (*left*) the library, spacious, elegant and markedly devoid of the Bohemian clutter favoured by Sullivan.

Gilbert's words. Wagner had stirred the Western world with a new kind of grand opera; Sullivan always said that *The Mastersingers of Nuremberg* was the greatest comic opera ever written. With Wagner the music came first.

But 1883 brought comforts to Sullivan's ego. On 13 May his forty-first birthday was celebrated at his home by a party including the Prince of Wales, the Duke of Edinburgh, various unoperatic peers, Millais, Gilbert, and Burnand, now editor of *Punch*. Tosti and Madame Albani sang, and then on this Sunday evening Sullivan sprang a surprise. D'Oyly Carte had assembled on the Savoy stage the cast of *Iolanthe*, surrounding the telephone, and exactly at 11.15 they began singing while two miles away Sullivan passed an earpiece from ear to astonished ear.

At Windsor Castle nine days later Sullivan was knighted by Queen Victoria, along with his old friend George Grove who had just become Director of the Royal College of Music. Almost at once the *Musical Review* remarked: 'Some things that Mr. Arthur Sullivan may do, Sir Arthur ought not to do. Here is not only an opportunity, but a positive obligation for him to return to the sphere from which he has too long descended.' This message hit Sullivan just when he was at cross-purposes with Gilbert over the ludicrous Lozenge, an idea that haunted the plot-book for years: by swallowing a lozenge (or other elixir) a character would be changed into another character, with incredible consequences. Sullivan refused to swallow

Richard Wagner (1813–83), whose music charmed, intrigued or scandalized the ears of Europe during the late nineteenth century. His complex compositions of 'endless melody' wrought a revolution in opera.

the Lozenge, it was 'too artificial'. Nor did he care, at first, for Gilbert's next idea of turning his old play *The Princess* into a comic opera, to be called *Princess Ida*. Sir Arthur Sullivan wanted to take wings and soar higher.

Why did not Sullivan follow the course the academics expected of him? Partly because Gilbert, to do him justice, sought to shape *Princess Ida* on less topsy-turvy lines; and partly because the normally genial streak in Sullivan could not resist comedy for long; also, highbrow music could not pay for the high life that Sullivan lived. The fee he received for conducting the 1883 Leeds Festival, three hundred guineas, was as much as he lost – or won – in a night at Monte Carlo. He knew that by composing another comic opera he could always refill his coffers, but this knowledge, comforting as it was financially, pricked his artistic conscience.

Gilbert's rehash of his old play about feminism was not W.S.G. at his topical best, for women were now taking degrees at several universities, and his fun with Princess Ida's college for ladies, to whom Man is strictly redundant, now seems less than emancipated ('And they're going to do without him, If they can – *if they can*!'). But beneath this Victorian badinage was a serious theme, and Gilbert was paradoxically a serious man: 'I can do something more than wear the cap and bells.' In *Princess Ida* he was, rather nervously, trying a recipe somewhat different from the mixture as before.

Here and there Sullivan's music tended towards that grand opera which in his heart of hearts he longed to compose, but in *Ida* the grander colours were laid modestly, in deference to Gilbert's insistence that music in comic opera must always be kept down so that not a word should be lost. Composition was pushed aside in October as Sir Arthur sped north to the Leeds Musical Festival.

Forty years before the birth of the BBC, some of the Festival concerts of 1883 were broadcast. This scientific feat caused a sensation in Yorkshire and beyond. The National Telephone Company was just beginning experiments in using telephone wires not only for personal conversations but for transmissions from halls, churches and theatres. A musical play was broadcast to London subscribers in 1883, and, having set up its Northern headquarters in Park Row, Leeds, the company installed ten telephones at various points around the Victoria Hall especially for the Musical Festival. When most of the 250 subscribers on the Leeds exchange asked to be connected it was found technically impracticable to transmit to all simultaneously, so they took turns twenty-five at a time. Listeners were able to sit in their homes, reported the *Yorkshire Post*, and hear 'grand interpretations' of sublime music! Subscribers in Bradford, Dewsbury, Huddersfield, Leeds and other West Riding towns enjoyed 'this privilege'. The company also invited a party of 'auditors' to its manager's office where they heard on headphones 'most distinctly'.

This was a pioneering event. Not until 1894, eleven years later, was the Electrophone Company founded expressly to provide such facilities in the main towns. To the National Telephone Company in 1883 the value of the exercise was mainly in publicity for the domestic telephone. But the wonder of it was recognized. Who would have believed, exclaimed the *Leeds Mercury*, that persons in Wakefield and elsewhere would be able to hear Sir Arthur Sullivan's 'magnificent chorus' many miles away?

The *Yorkshire Post*'s reference to Sullivan's 'grand interpretations' was significant, for this year's Leeds Festival, though lacking the proposed Sullivan symphony, saw his credit rise higher than ever as an interpreter of great music. His conducting of Beethoven's *Mass in D* was considered the best performance ever heard in England. He always enjoyed himself at Leeds. His enthusiasm and musicianship had moved mountains since those early days when as a young man he set out to travel the land with his baton; he had raised the standard of good music among the artisans and business people of the provinces. In his choirs the mill-hands and mill-owners, the shop assistants and shop-owners, the clerks and businessmen rubbed shoulders, and they sang with the greatest soloists in the land. Sullivan called the 1883 Festival 'the most sublime' ever, then rushed back to London, to a fight against time and his health. He flogged himself to complete *Princess Ida* for the première advertised for 5 January 1884.

Final rehearsals lasted until 2.30 a.m. on the day when the public were to be admitted. Sullivan collapsed at home and was told not to get up again. Cautious Carte had meanwhile had slips printed, regretting that the composer was unable to conduct. But, fortified with morphine and black coffee, Sullivan drove to the theatre 'more dead than alive', his diary tells. 'Tremendous house – usual reception. . . . Brilliant success. After performance I turned faint and could not stand.'

Three weeks later the Savoy management received a letter from Sullivan saying that he would write no more comic operas. Optimistically, Carte hoped the decision would be reversed when Sullivan returned from convalescence in France. Gilbert, pessimistically alarmed by some unusually hostile first-night criticisms (it was 'from every point of view the weakest' of their operas, said *Figaro*), ordered the box office to telephone the takings every night, using a code to avoid phone-tapping:

F A V O U R I T E S

1   2   3   4   5   6   7   8   9   0

'In telephoning (say) £256,' he explained to Carte, 'the clerk with say A U R pounds; so £128 would be F A T (but not very fat) and so on.' By March there was so little fat that Carte sent the collaborators six months' notice of a new opera being required. This was in accordance with their five-year contract.

Sullivan reiterated his resolution never to write 'anything of the character of those already written by Gilbert and myself'. Expressing astonishment, Gilbert wrote to Sullivan: 'I have invariably subordinated my views to your own.' To Sullivan this was carrying Gilbertian topsy-turvydom into their own relationship. The music, he replied from Paris, was never allowed to arise and speak for itself. Such subordination was most disheartening to the composer: 'I want a chance for the music to act in its own proper sphere.' He urged that they try a story of human interest, not one of Gilbertian improbability. *Reality* in plot and character would bring fresh vitality to their joint work.

Reality! – Gilbert retorted: 'You teach me the A B C of my profession. It is inconceivable that any sane author should ever write otherwise than as you

Telephone subscribers enjoying a relay from a theatre, 1898. The significance of the Leeds experiment in 'broadcasting' may be judged by the fact that it was several years before the Electrophone Company introduced a similar service to the capital.

A scene from the first performance of *Princess Ida*.

propose I should write in future.' This clash alarmed Carte, who was gravely concerned about what to do when *Princess Ida* closed, as soon it must, but he took comfort in Gilbert's assurance that he already had a new libretto sketched out. As soon as Sullivan was back in London Gilbert drove to see him and presented – the Lozenge, revised version. It was rejected. Gilbert left in pained incomprehension. For days Carte shuttled, peace-making, from one to the other; then Sullivan wrote a conciliatory letter to Gilbert asking why should they not try something *quite new*? Unhappily, the olive branch reached Gilbert just when he was putting in some further revision on the Lozenge. He answered: 'I cannot consent to construct another plot for the next opera.' Sullivan replied: 'The tone of your letter convinces me that your decision is final and therefore further discussion is useless. I regret it very much.' *Princess Ida* closed after 246 performances – not bad for a rehash. But no new opera was in preparation.

It seemed like the end of a great partnership. A day or so later Gilbert was striding up and down his study, fuming at the impasse, when a huge Japanese sword decorating the wall fell with a clatter to the floor. 'It suggested the broad idea,' as he said later. His journalistic mind, always quick to seize on topicalities, turned to a Japanese Exhibition recently opened in the neigh-bourhood. Little Japanese men and women from the Japanese village at the Exhibition attracted every eye as they walked through the streets of Knightsbridge in their Oriental robes, and Gilbert knew very well how, as Japan Westernized herself, her art was influencing the French Impressionists and such London artists as Whistler. Japanese prints were in vogue. Now he sat at his desk and opened his plot-book at a fresh page. If the Japanese could Westernize themselves, how about Japanizing the English? 'In this play', wrote G. K. Chesterton of *The Mikado*, 'Gilbert pursued and persecuted the evils of modern England till they had literally not a leg to stand on, exactly as Swift did under the allegory of *Gulliver's Travels*. I doubt if there is a single joke in the whole play that fits the Japanese. But all the jokes in the play fit the English.'

Gilbert sent a summary of the idea to Sullivan who replied immediately with his 'inexpressible relief' at 'a plot without the supernatural and improbable'. All unpleasantness was ended. The new opera was destined to be the most valuable theatre property in the world. Many people consider it the brightest jewel of all in the Savoy casket. Certainly this is the biggest Gilbertian joke of all: that the plot which was *not* to deal with 'the improbable' should be of all Gilbert's grotesqueries the most far-fetched, this English Never-Never-Land thinly disguised as Japan and filled with the wildest caricatures of humanity.

It is remarkable how many things of value and significance to us today are the harvest of a great outburst of productivity in the period 1884–85. Daimler invented the petrol engine. Gold was discovered in the Transvaal. The Fabian Society was founded in England. One of its founders, George Bernard Shaw, was writing his first play. Charles Parsons invented the steam turbine. Kipling was about to emerge as the Bard of Empire. *Parsifal*, which had its first British performance at the Albert Hall (Sullivan thought it 'gloomy, dull and ugly'), brought the Wagnerian revolution to an end. *The Mikado* was not the end of Gilbert and Sullivan, but it did mark an all-round consummation of that revolution in the light musical theatre which they had started with *Thespis* fourteen years earlier. *The Mikado*'s first night at the Savoy on 14 March 1885 was met with unanimous approval and delight. This opera played in every part of the English-speaking world; four D'Oyly Carte companies toured the British Isles; one was sent to France, Holland, Austria-Hungary and Germany, where the Emperor attended a performance in Berlin. If this pleased the socialite in Sullivan, as doubtless it did, the composer Sullivan was doubly pleased by the *Neue Musik-Zeitung*'s verdict that *The Mikado* contained music of an extraordinary richness and quality unknown in German operettas.

With one curious exception (the authentically Japanese chorus 'Miya Sama', to which the imperial army reputedly marched to battle in 1868), the music of the opera follows an essentially English idiom. To have filled *The Mikado* with pseudo-Japanese tunes would have weakened the fun made of England in that familiar-yet-unfamiliar town of Titipu where the Lord High Executioner arrives to a tune no more Oriental than 'A Fine Old English Gentleman', to which it bears a resemblance. The Lord High Everything Else, Pooh-Bah, though attired as a tremendously swell Japanese, is the compromising politician of any nationality. There is true English sentiment in the exquisite soprano aria 'The sun whose rays are all ablaze'.

Punch's view of Mr Carte, 1882.

The Mikado: the English japanned.
(Above) Photograph taken by Gilbert
at the Japanese Exhibition in London in 1884, and doubtless used by
him as reference material for his new
opera. (Above right) The 'Three Little
Maids' of the first production – critics
complained that the costumes im-
parted 'to the prettiest girl's figure
the seeming of a bolster loosely
wrapped up in a dressing gown'.
(Right) Advertisement issued by
Liberty's, the Regent Street store
which led the field for aesthetic and
other unusual draperies and supplied
some of the costumes for The Mikado.

A modern production of *The Mikado*, and (*left*) costume designs by Charles Ricketts for the 1926 D'Oyly Carte production.

There is English brutality in the Mikado's obsession with punishment ('something lingering, with boiling oil in it') and with public decapitation. Gilbert said he could not bear to crush a beetle under his boot, but many of his fellow countrymen enjoyed cock-fights, rat-fights, human kick-shins, and other brutal sports; lavish newspaper coverage of sordid crimes is evidence of Victorian morbidity, and the last public execution in England had been only seventeen years before.

Having decided upon the Japanese camouflage for his satire, Gilbert went to infinite pains to perfect it. Eleven times he rewrote the plot. The principal artists wore genuine Japanese costumes of ancient date. Antique suits of armour were brought from Japan, only to be found useless because they would not fit any man taller than five feet four inches. Carte printed in *The Mikado* programme an acknowledgment to the 'Directors and Inhabitants of the Japanese Village': W.S.G. had brought geisha girls from there to his rehearsals to teach deportment and the spreading and snapping of fans to denote wrath, delight or homage.

The unusual hiatus after *Princess Ida*'s close had caused widespread conjecture in the press about its successor, and anxiety made Gilbert for once unsure of his judgment; at rehearsal he even cut the Mikado's now famous song 'My object all sublime', only to reinstate it in response to a petition from the choristers. During the performance Gilbert tramped the Thames Embankment: 'Agony and apprehension possessed me.' He returned to take a footlight ovation alongside Sullivan, whose diary adds: 'Seven encores taken – might have taken eleven.' This first London run of *The Mikado* lasted nearly two years (672 performances) and the Savoyards' kingdom became worldwide as pesos, marks, francs, and dollars poured into their coffers.

With such a money-spinner at stake the fight against American piracy went to astonishing lengths. When the opera was in preparation one New York management sent a spy to London; Carte promptly hired detectives to report what piratical managements were cooking up in the States. The first to open an alleged *Mikado* in New York was roasted by the *New York Herald*'s critic, who understood what Gilbert and Sullivan stood for, 'but as here presented it was butchered, botched, mauled and mangled'. Carte smuggled across the Atlantic an entire *Mikado* company, pre-rehearsed and travelling in total secrecy; they figured in the liner's passenger list under assumed names, with D'Oyly Carte as Henry Chapman. In this way the authentic *Mikado* was able to steal priority from the most formidable of the New York pirates, who was still in rehearsal when the D'Oyly Carte company opened at the Fifth Avenue Theatre. There they ran 430 performances, while probably a hundred pirated versions across the States did their worst: one transferred *The Mikado* to Balmoral Castle where Queen Victoria was shown as a whisky addict and Prince of Wales Nanki-Poo's lady friend was named Langtry-Poo. D'Oyly Carte retaliated by sending five more companies to tour the USA and Canada in 1886 with the genuine article.

Back in London, Carte ran into trouble with Gilbert. Suspicious or jealous of the degree of Carteian control at the Savoy Theatre, he trotted out an absurd scheme for tripartite daily management. 'I can't see how you and

More than any other of the operas, *The Mikado* went on to endure an endless variety of travesties and 'updated renderings', including 'Hot', Folies Bergère, ballet, film and 'Swing' versions, especially after the expiry of the Gilbert and Sullivan copyright in 1961. In some modern productions, however, such as those of the Sadler's Wells company in London, the impact of fresh interpretation has done nothing but good to the operas' reputation.

Self-caricature by W.S.G., scrawled all over with such sentiments as 'I like pinching little babies' and 'Confound everything!'

Sullivan are part-managers of the theatre,' wrote Carte, 'any more than I am part-author or part-composer of the music.' In a huff Gilbert said he was being treated merely as a hack-writer, and to Sullivan he insisted that they should share in the management of the theatre, because if Carte were left alone and unfettered, he might do ill-advised things and ruin the business.

Carte replied: 'Of course you run this risk. But my reply is that I stand the whole risk of pecuniary loss' – for by their contract the three partners shared equally the profits of the operas at the Savoy, but not any losses. Sullivan indicated firmly that he was very happy with Carte's management. Gilbert subsided but this affair is significant of the trend in their relationship towards Gilbert versus Carte-Sullivan.

The Ironmaster at the Savoy.

Cartoon of Gilbert which clearly alludes to his indefatigable campaign to raise production standards in the Victorian theatre.

That Gilbert as producer was unquestioned master over the presentation on the stage was not yet in dispute. A long run such as *The Mikado* enjoyed is apt to lure the best of players into moods of slackness and of irresponsibility, so every now and then W.S.G. would drop in at the Savoy to check up on discipline:

'I am told, Mr Grossmith, that in last night's performance when you and Miss Bond were kneeling before the Mikado she gave you a push and you rolled completely over on the floor.'

'Yes. You see, I – in my interpretation of Ko-Ko –'

'Whatever your interpretation, please omit that in future.'

'Certainly if you wish it, but I got a big laugh by it.'

'So you would if you sat on a pork pie.'

The pork pie represents Gilbert's attitude to all the English theatre's slapstick burlesque which his subtler methods of acting and wording had surpassed. But *parodying* the old-fashioned theatre he was quite prepared to do, and this was the next idea he unfolded o Sullivan early in 1886, an operatic send-up of Victorian blood-and-thunder melodrama, complete with a wicked baronet, Sir Despard Murgatroyd, whose ancestors step down from their frames and threaten him with 'ruddy gore' should he hesitate to commit his daily crime. But getting the music composed was another matter. Sullivan had already started setting Longfellow's *The Golden Legend* as an oratorio for the Leeds Festival in October. And the venerable Franz Liszt was paying London a visit, so Sullivan had to entertain him at a round of functions. And everywhere in Society Sullivan in his turn was shown off by the elegant Mrs Ronalds – at race-meetings in the spring, yachting at Cowes in the summer, at garden-parties, at concerts and theatres she loved to parade her lion. All that summer Sullivan had to compose the music for two utterly different works side by side. 'How am I to get through this year's work? Do they think me a barrel-organ? They turn a handle and I disgorge music of any mood to order.' So came *The Golden Legend*. In the *Yorkshire Post*'s opinion, 'On no former occasion has the world-renowned Leeds chorus met together with stronger determination to achieve honour for itself, its work, and its conductor, than on the last morning of the Festival week.'

Sullivan's oratorio ended with audience and orchestra leaping to their feet, cheering and pelting the conductor-composer with flowers. The critics were unanimous. *The Times* said: 'The Leeds Festival may boast of having given life to a work which, if not one of genius in the strict sense of the word, is at least likely to survive till our long expected English Beethoven appears on the scene.' This proved to be a shrewd judgment, for Sullivan's serious music lasted only until Elgar's displaced it. The *World* went so far as to label Sullivan 'the Mozart of England'. Some years later Sullivan himself took the heat out of such adulation: recalling that during the same 1886 Festival he had conducted Bach's *Mass in B Minor* (its first English performance was only ten years earlier in London), he said that he would have given his all to have composed just the Sanctus in that great work.

Ruddygore had a mixed reception in January 1887 at the Savoy, its audience split between those who hissed and shouted 'Give us back *The Mikado*' and those who cheered; and then there was the embarrassment of the title. To

Sullivan as a pillar of the musical
Establishment: (*above*) in a group
with Franz Liszt during the Hun-
garian composer's visit to London in
1886 – also in the group are the
celebrated violinist Joachim (shaking
the Abbé's hand) and Charles Hallé
(far right); (*right*) at that year's Leeds
Musical Festival – other figures
illustrated include Antonin
Dvořák (present to conduct his
St Ludmila), Madame Albani
and Alderman Fred Spark, the
Secretary of the Festival.

Gilbert at first resisted pressure to change the title of his new opera, suggesting in exasperation that it be renamed *Kensington Gore: or Not so Good as The Mikado*.

A contemporary artist's impression of Richard Temple as Sir Roderick Murgatroyd singing 'The Ghost's High Noon', a song in which Sullivan indulged his yearning to write music that made a stronger contribution to the operas.

Gilbert ruddy gore simply meant melodramatic red blood. The *Graphic* thought the title all right for men but it would 'scarcely sound pretty on ladies' lips'. A man at Gilbert's club asked: 'How is *Bloodygore* going on?' 'It isn't *Bloodygore*, it's *Ruddygore*,' the author responded. 'Oh, it's the same thing.' 'Is it? Then I suppose you'll take it that if I say "I admire your ruddy countenance," I mean "I like your bloody cheek!"' But within a few days Gilbert changed the '*y*' to '*i*'.

Ruddigore was not, as Jeremiahs had prophesied, a failure. It ran 288 performances, and Gilbert remarked: 'I could do with a few more such failures.' But it was not another *Mikado*. The partners were both dissatisfied. Here and there Sullivan let loose his propensity for grand opera, notably in a chorus sung by the ghostly baronets as they step from their frames – one of Gilbert's finest lyrics:

> *When the night wind howls in the chimney cowls,*
> *and the bat in the moonlight flies,*
> *And inky clouds, like funeral shrouds,*
> *sail over the midnight skies. . . .*

and so on in macabre description, matched splendidly by Sullivan's evocative orchestration. Yet Gilbert wrote afterwards: 'That music seems to my uninstructed ear to be very fine indeed, but out of place in a comic opera. It is as though one inserted fifty lines of *Paradise Lost* into a farcical comedy.' Some critics took the opposite line, accusing Sullivan of prostituting his art in the 'trivial' *Ruddigore*. Sir Arthur escaped to the Riviera, to sunshine and casinos, and to Berlin to conduct *The Golden Legend* at a gala performance for Kaiser William I's ninetieth birthday – but when he was presented to the royal family in the palace the Kaiser's band played a selection from *The Mikado*! The dichotomy in Sullivan's aspirations was never more pronounced.

When he returned to England, to the blazing summer of Queen Victoria's Jubilee, he was asked by the Prince of Wales to compose an Ode for one of its many celebrations. This was very much to Sir Arthur Sullivan's taste. He sat down to write the 'Jubilee Ode'; all 'trivial' music was put out of his thoughts. Gilbert wrote to Carte: 'He ought to attend to business a little.' When they met Sullivan, Gilbert suggested the Lozenge; Sullivan wearily agreed to 'a sort of provisional compromise' whereby Gilbert was to write part of the Lozenge opera and if it still proved unacceptable 'no more should be said about it'. But four months later when the two met again Sullivan rejected it once and for all. 'It is a puppet show, and not human. It is impossible to feel any sympathy with a single person. I don't see my way to setting it in its present form.'

When a mere revival of *H.M.S. Pinafore* stopped the gap at the Savoy people shook their heads. No new 'G and S'? It seemed incredible amid the Jubilee-promoted state of euphoria in Britain. The old Queen had emerged from seclusion to take part in the jubilations and her people had realized to what power and influence Britain had grown during her reign. Their troops and colonists had recently occupied Burma and Egypt. India and Africa had been 'opened up'. At home 'the development of railways, steam-navigation, and

electricity is the work of our time,' said a proud *Times* leader. Shutting an eye
to the dark working-class side of industrialization, the expansionists looked
across the oceans for new markets: 'Trade follows the flag.' Not since Queen
Elizabeth's reign had there been such imperialist fervour as now, in the high
Victorian summer before the decline and decadence of the 1890s. Their Drakes
and Raleighs were now Empire-builders, such men as Cecil Rhodes.

Sir Arthur Sullivan took a refreshingly independent line, in contrast to the
prevailing materialist glory-making, when he spoke at Birmingham on why
Britain had *lost* her leading world position in music for nearly two centuries:
'This was largely due to the enthusiasm with which commerce was pursued,
and to the extraordinary way in which religious and political struggles, and,
later still, practical science, have absorbed our energies. . . . Now, however,
the conditions of things is changing – it *has* changed. And yet I cannot but
feel that we are only at the entry of the Promised Land. Habits of mind and
modes of action are still to be found which show that we have much to do
before we become the musical people that we were in the remoter ages of
our history.'

This remarkable insight comes from a musician to whom England owes
a debt – not generally recognized – for the leading part he played in reviving

At the climax of a reign during
which Britain had risen to a position
of unparalleled power and prosperity,
the seventy-eight-year-old Queen
Victoria is driven in procession to
St Paul's for the Thanksgiving service on the occasion of her Diamond
Jubilee, 22 June 1897.

her native tradition in music; he made this contribution both as a conductor of festivals and as a composer of comic operas in which one may trace a heritage of song going back to the Tudors, especially pronounced in Sullivan's graceful madrigals. For a widening public he opened the way to the Promised Land of Elgar, Vaughan Williams, Holst and Britten.

The Times declared in 1887: 'the middle classes and even the working classes, which had no opportunity of appreciating either art or music fifty years ago, cannot now complain that these wholesome enjoyments are mono-polised by a fashionable aristocracy.' Gilbert as well as Sullivan would have been less than human had he not reflected on how much 'wholesome enjoy-ment' they had created together, but he was saddened, too, for he was sensitive to their separation. One morning, waiting for a train on Uxbridge Station, he found himself staring at the Tower Furnishing Company's poster depicting the Tower of London. In Victoria's Jubilee year, with its strain of a revivified Elizabethan spirit, it was small wonder that Gilbert should draft in his plot-book a Tudor story called *The Tower Warder*. The wonder comes in his change of attitude towards working with Sullivan. On Christmas morning 1887 the three partners met at Sullivan's rooms: 'Gilbert read plot of new piece (Tower of London) – immensely pleased with it. Pretty story, no topsy-turvydom, very human and funny also.' No Lozenge. They agreed that *The Yeomen of the Guard* (as it was eventually named) should be sub-titled 'A new and original opera' – the term 'comic opera' was dropped.

For months Gilbert was absorbed in Tudor England. He went to the Tower of London to sense its atmosphere, and to sketch its 'Beefeaters'. In this opera, for the first time, he was not tilting at anything. It is a tragic story, with comic interludes, of Jack Point the jester who goes with a troupe of strolling players to the Tower of London where he loses his sweetheart to Colonel Fairfax. Point's broken-hearted 'I have a song to sing, O' is rooted in the English folk-song tradition. In *The Yeomen* Sullivan and Gilbert created a tapestry of sixteenth-century England more serious and poetic than anything of theirs before. Years later, when a monument to Sir Arthur Sullivan was erected in the Embankment Gardens, Gilbert chose from *The Yeomen* the words that are carved on it:

> *Is life a boon?*
> *If so, it must befall*
> *That Death, when e'er he call*
> *Must call too soon. . . .*

Sullivan in 1888 welcomed this more serious vein. He later described *The Yeomen* as the best of all his works with Gilbert, but in the spring months when Gilbert was engaged on the text Sir Arthur was on the Riviera, worried by his health and by the consequences of *Dorothy*. This comic opera by Alfred Cellier was drawing enormous crowds to the Gaiety Theatre – eventually it ran for more performances (931) than any Gilbert and Sullivan opera. Sullivan's reaction was that, because other men were now exploiting a field which had been his own, the time had certainly come for him to leave it altogether. He was influenced not only by *Dorothy*: Carl Rosa was putting

Sketch of a 'Beefeater' by Gilbert.

on English grand opera (such as it was) at Drury Lane. This, surely, should be his own new field. Sullivan was also impressed by Carte who said that their strategy should be to raise their own Savoy standards far above *Dorothy*'s and Carl Rosa's by building a larger theatre, recruiting an even better company, and 'making a fresh start'. After all, Gilbert's *Yeomen* conception pointed in that direction.

From Monte Carlo Sullivan sent to Gilbert his blessing on Carte's great scheme. The reply was a splendid piece of rhetorical common sense: 'Why in the world we are to throw up the sponge and begin all over again because *Dorothy* has run 500 nights beats my comprehension. . . . We have the best theatre, the best company, the best composer, and (though I say it) the best librettist in England working together – we are world-known, and as much an institution as Westminster Abbey – and to scatter this splendid organisation because *Dorothy* has run 500 nights is, to my way of thinking, to give up a gold mine. What is *Dorothy*'s success to us? It is not even the same class of piece as ours.'

Gilbert was annoyed to find Carte and Sullivan putting their heads together. Carte himself was in no mood to placate Gilbert, having just had a squabble with him at a rehearsal of a stop-gap *Pirates of Penzance*, when Carte

The Yeomen of the Guard: (*left*) Rhoda Maitland as Elsie and Henry Lytton as Jack Point in an 1888 provincial tour. It was Lytton who first interpreted Point's death as unrelievedly tragic – an innovation which Gilbert did not resist, his initial anxiety about the opera's seriousness having somewhat waned. (*Above*) Richard Temple as Meryll in the original production.

accused Gilbert of wasting everyone's time. W.S.G.'s mastership over the stage was disputed. Carte cabled to Sullivan: 'Serious row with author don't really see how things are to go on.' But two days later: 'Row made up all is peace.' The Carte-Sullivan friendship was underlined when Sir Arthur returned to London for Richard D'Oyly Carte's wedding to Helen Lenoir at the Savoy Chapel: Sullivan was best man. Carte's first wife had died three years previously. With his ex-secretary Helen, partner now in life as in business, he set up a new London home at 4 Adelphi Terrace. Ever in the advance guard of every movement for the sophisticated amenities of life, Carte installed a lift – a rarity in a private house – and he invited his friend Whistler to help decorate the lovely old Adam house. Whistler left the Adam features untouched but prescribed a Whistlerian colour scheme: 'His idea was to make the house gay and delicate in colour,' said Mrs Carte. The library, for instance, was in primrose-yellow 'as if the sun was shining, however dark the day'.

D'Oyly Carte was building a luxurious hotel close to the Savoy Theatre. He recruited Sullivan as a director of the hotel company, not Gilbert. His ideas were again ahead of their time – there were so many bathrooms that the builder asked: 'Do you think your guests are going to be amphibious?'

The casino at Monte Carlo, haunt of Sir Arthur Sullivan during his many visits to the Riviera in search of health and distraction.

At the Savoy Hotel (opened 1889) Carte, the inventor of the after-theatre supper, set up new gastronomic standards for London hotels with the same flair for the good and the profitable as he had applied to new artistic standards in theatres.

A month after the Carte wedding a royal command performance of *The Golden Legend* at the Albert Hall came to a momentous conclusion for Sullivan when he hurried to Her Majesty's presence, and heard her say: 'You ought to write a grand opera, Sir Arthur, you would do it so well.' It was as good as a command. Long ago Rachel Scott Russell had urged him; he had kept putting off *the* great work of his life; now he knew it was irresistible – especially as D'Oyly Carte's architects were planning an ambitious theatre to be built in Cambridge Circus, to be called the Royal English Opera House (now the Palace Theatre).

But the immediate task was to complete *The Yeomen of the Guard*. Most of the music was composed at Fleet in Hampshire. Sullivan proved himself more

James McNeill Whistler and (*left*) the sketch he made from D'Oyly Carte's office window of the scaffolding going up on the site of the new Savoy Hotel in 1888. Whistler characteristically remarked at the time that the hotel would never look so well again.

The Gondoliers takes shape. (*Above*) Notes in Gilbert's plot-book for his stage directions for the game of blind man's buff; (*opposite above*) a contemporary view of the scene as it was eventually played at the Savoy, and (*below*) part of Sullivan's score.

way home. When he heard that Gilbert's new plot was set in Venice, Sullivan's interest lit up; having recently been there himself he could visualize the operatic possibilities. At this Paris meeting Sullivan also agreed that the grand opera to open Carte's new theatre would be his setting of Scott's *Ivanhoe*, thus committing himself to write a grand opera and a comic opera at the same time, just as Gilbert had suggested. But he still insisted that in comic opera his music must be more prominent; the opening of *The Gondoliers* is a continuous cascade of music unbroken by dialogue for some eighteen minutes, music which brilliantly builds that exuberant scene on the Piazzetta at Venice in 1750; and throughout the opera Sullivan's contribution is by no means subordinate. It was a very human twist of Sullivan's psychology that as soon as he was actually writing a grand opera for the Royal English Opera House back came his old zest for comic opera at the Savoy.

The Gondoliers is a joyous opera, happy, kindly, exuberant, the sweet fruit of reconciliation after the bitter quarrel. And in it there is a reflection of the Gilbert-Sullivan personal situation, for in *The Gondoliers* there appear two humble gondoliers of Venice, Marco and Guiseppe, one of whom is the only son of the late King of Barataria but until the end of the opera we don't know which is which, so 'I have arranged that you will reign jointly,' says the Grand Inquisitor, Don Alhambra del Bolero, 'so that no question can arise hereafter as to the validity of your acts.'

Likewise, Messrs Gilbert and Sullivan reigned jointly over *The Gondoliers*, creating it as 'master and master'. On a May day in 1889, Sullivan's diary records, they 'shook hands and buried the hatchet'. Through the summer

The basic situation in *The Gondoliers* displayed ironic similarities to the state of its creators' relationship, a fact that was not lost on *Punch*.

Sullivan composed *The Gondoliers* at a riverside house at Weybridge. Gilbert maintained a shuttle service of lyrics with obliging notes such as: 'Dear Sullivan – will this do? If it don't, then send it back and I'll try again. Yours very truly, W.S.G.' The original idea of the plot was borrowed from a history of Venetian Republicans in the fifteenth century (updated by Gilbert to the eighteenth). Guying republicanism had a mild topical interest, since the French Revolution was fresh in many memories, but the left wing was of such small account in Britain – Keir Hardie had started the Scottish Labour Party only in the previous year – that *Gondoliers* audiences took the opera as it was meant, as a frolic remote from daily life.

Composing *Ivanhoe* with his other hand, Sullivan had an exceedingly busy year. He directed the Leeds Festival in October, though he failed to provide a

'Leeds Symphony' as invited (he toyed with *The Dream of Gerontius* as an oratorio subject but left it for Elgar to compose a decade later); then in November back to *The Gondoliers*. Its Venetian setting brought out the gayest response from Sullivan's Italian blood. This Mediterranean quality conceals amazingly Sullivan's private agony. His diary is now milestoned with pathetic little entries: 'Very seedy all day.... Too tired to go to rehearsal. ... Home very tired.... Only slept an hour.'

Yet in *one* such night he composed 'Take a Pair of Sparkling Eyes' and the jaunty 'There lived a King, as I've been told, in the wonder-working days of old', and rewrote two other numbers. This sort of thing scared Gilbert and D'Oyly Carte, both for Sullivan's sake and for the opera. Gilbert wanted it postponed. Fortunately the Savoy box office perked up; *The Yeomen of the Guard* ran for a year and a quarter until it gave way to its successor on 7 December 1889.

'The Gondoliers a Great Success' headlined the *Sunday Times* next day. 'May it go forth to the world that the distinguished collaborators to whom the present generation is indebted for some of its most delightful entertainment have scored a great triumph.' The Savoy Theatre rocked with delight at the vivacious climax, the cachuca sung and danced by the entire company, a side-issue of which was noted by the *Topical Times*: 'The chorus wore comparatively short skirts for the first time, and the gratifying fact is revealed to a curious world that the Savoy chorus are a very well-legged lot.' More dignified critics extolled the musicianly humour of *The Gondoliers*, as exemplified in the cross-rhythms of the quartet 'In a contemplative fashion'.

Next day Gilbert wrote to Sullivan: 'I must thank you for the magnificent work you have put into the piece. It gives one the chance of shining right through the twentieth century with a reflected light.' And Sullivan replied: 'Don't talk of reflected light. In such a perfect book as *The Gondoliers* you shine with an individual brilliancy which no other writer can hope to attain.'

The *Daily Telegraph* said so rightly: '*The Gondoliers* conveys an impression of having been written *con amore*.' So the year 1889 went out in a blaze of amity.

Yet within nine months the Savoy Trinity were at loggerheads in the law courts. The dismal Carpet Quarrel has been rehashed many times; it is sufficient in our present purpose of studying the relationship of Gilbert and Sullivan to their world to record a few of the world's reactions to the quarrel. In the spring of 1890 Sullivan was at Weybridge working contentedly on *Ivanhoe* when his peace was shattered by a letter from Gilbert who on returning from a holiday in India had been 'appalled' to learn from Carte that the cost of mounting *The Gondoliers* had been 'the stupendous sum of £4,500', of which, he said, 'the most surprising item was £500 for new carpets' at the front of the Savoy Theatre. (The actual cost of the accursed carpet was £140!) The tripartite agreement of 1883 had provided that the three men shared the profits of the operas equally, after deduction of 'repairs incidental to the performance'. Gilbert, the one-time barrister, now contended that a carpet could not be a repair. In conference at the theatre Carte replied that wear-and-tear expenditure was customarily charged to any person renting a theatre. Gilbert snapped: 'You're making too much money out of my brains,' and when – to Gilbert's surprise – Sullivan sided with Carte he called them both blackguards and rushed from the room. He wrote to Sullivan: 'The time for putting an end to our partnership has at last arrived.' When this affair, with its lawyers' brew of complications, reached the courts Sullivan was more shocked than the others by 'seeing our names coupled in hostile antagonism over a few miserable pounds'. So was their devoted public. The London *Star*: 'Sir Arthur did not want to quarrel with Mr Carte or anyone else. He declined to quarrel with Mr Carte. Consequently he got into a quarrel with Mr Gilbert.' The *New York World*: 'What a niggard Nature is in not making Gilbert and Sullivan one person – a sort of Lord High Everything Else of comic opera! Then they might have quarrelled as much as they pleased without eclipsing the gaiety of nations.' When the lawyers disclosed that each of the partners had collected £90,000 in eleven years, the *Musical Times* remarked: 'Human nature cannot stand such prosperity without arriving at the point where it is prepared to make a *casus belli* out of a carpet.'

Up and down the said carpet thronged the contented audiences of *The Gondoliers* until its long run (554 performances) ended in the midsummer of 1891 – with no new 'G and S'. Meanwhile Sullivan had experienced the exquisite balm to his wounds of seeing his grand opera performed to open Carte's new theatre on 31 January 1891. On the morning of that day Gilbert received a letter from Sullivan: 'Let your presence at the theatre tonight be an intimation that you are as ready and willing as I am to think no more of what has happened. . . . The enclosed stalls are not what I should have liked to send you, but the Royalties have taken two boxes out of six.' (Mrs Ronalds held court in another.) The enclosed tickets were not used. To Gilbert's legalistic mind, his wrongs were not yet righted.

Ivanhoe has been called the greatest non-event in Sullivan's life – and surely in D'Oyly Carte's. Every member of the *Ivanhoe* audience was given a printed statement of Carte's policy, 'To establish English Grand Opera'. He threw everything into this worthy and expensive venture: the best-equipped theatre in England, splendid scenery and costumes, a hamperful of gold in singers, the largest orchestra Sullivan had ever employed in a theatre (sixty-three players), a Carteian fanfare of publicity – everything but a Verdi or a Wagner as composer.

The critics were divided. George Bernard Shaw disliked Sullivan's 'gentlemanly' music and remarked in the *World* that 'it really does not do to spread butter on both sides of the bread', in reference to the advance publicity's tendency to equate Sullivan with Mozart. But Debussy likened the Sullivan of *Ivanhoe* to Massenet, and many London critics praised it. *Ivanhoe* ran 155 performances, but with waning attendance. When it came off Sullivan's one grand opera retired into oblivion, and nothing British followed it. There *were* no British Verdis or Wagners. Today some musicologists (notably Dr Percy Young) consider that, like some other works by the 'serious' Sullivan, *Ivanhoe* had passages of fine quality but that its composer lacked consistency of inspiration on this high level. D'Oyly Carte, too, had made a misjudgment: the British musical climate was not set for a renaissance of grand opera in the 1890s. 'Carte's Folly', as the City called it, was sold for use as a music-hall; renamed the Palace, its climate was brisk. Gilbert's earlier judgment that its

Rebecca defying the Templar, a scene from *Ivanhoe* which reflects the influence on Sullivan of the grand opera of Verdi and Wagner in this, his only attempt to emulate their high operatic seriousness.

site was bad for an opera house was proved correct. When he heard that Sullivan was disappointed by *Ivanhoe*'s semi-success he said: 'He's the sort of man who will sit on a fire and then complain that his bottom is burning.'

Gilbert has often been quoted as asserting a dislike of serious music, especially grand opera, but we may now see this as a professional front presented in order to resist efforts to involve him in a field of no commercial interest to him rather than as a true expression of his personal taste. For Mr Brian Rust, the gramophone historian, has discovered a hoard of records bought by W.S.G. in the early years of the twentieth century: they are all of grand opera.

There was a Gilbertian irony in the fact that Queen Victoria, who had given Sullivan a royal push to write grand opera, never saw *Ivanhoe* (though she sent to 'dear Sir Arthur' a message conveying her pleasure at reading of

The royal command performance of *The Gondoliers* at Windsor Castle, March 1891. 'Everybody was much pleased,' the Queen noted in her diary.

its 'great success' in the papers), but while it was running she ordered a command performance at Windsor of – *The Gondoliers*. This was first suggested in a letter from the Duke of Edinburgh to Sullivan, who replied from Monte Carlo that he had left England 'to get away from work and all the small worries and anxieties that are inherent in every important undertaking'. He promised to ask D'Oyly Carte to contact Windsor Castle 'as to the best means of carrying out Her Majesty's most gracious and flattering wish. . . . It will be very easy to run the Company down to Windsor in the afternoon and bring them back in time for the evening performance at the Savoy.' This letter is in the Royal Archives at Windsor; there is no correspondence with Gilbert. He and Sullivan were not present on the evening when the Queen wrote in her diary: 'The music, which I know and am fond of, is quite charming throughout and was well acted and sung. . . . Afterwards I spoke to Mr D'Oyly Carte and complimented him.'

Gilbert and Carte meanwhile continued to rub salt into their wounds by wearisome postal repetitions of insulting phrases about that carpet, etc., with a few Gilbertian barbs reserved for Sullivan. It was the music publisher Tom Chappell and, especially, the persuasive Helen D'Oyly Carte who brought about an armistice, disturbed at first by a few final fire-crackers from Gilbert. At about the same time the stage properties of *The Yeomen of the Guard* were put up for auction at the Savoy and Gilbert bought, of all things, the executioner's axe and block, writing (sardonically?) to Helen Carte: 'I should like to have them as a relic of the best of our joint work together.' Within a month of refusing Sullivan's *Ivanhoe* tickets he went to see the opera, and wrote: 'I am, as you know, quite unable to appreciate high-class music, and I expected to be bored – and I was not. This is the highest compliment I have ever paid a grand opera.' He addressed this compliment not to Sullivan but to Mrs Carte, for whom W.S.G. had a great regard.

Soon came reconciliation. Mr Gilbert withdrew insults; Mr Carte admitted a few 'unintentional overcharges' in the theatre accounts; Sir Arthur brought his sense of humour into a singularly humourless situation: 'Let us meet and shake hands. We can dispel the clouds hanging over us by setting up a counter-irritant in the form of a cloud of smoke.' Meeting at Sullivan's rooms, they agreed in principle on a new comic opera (*Utopia Limited*), but the composer asked that his work on it be deferred until his immediate commitments were completed. D'Oyly Carte had tried to team him with two rising young writers, J.M. Barrie and Conan Doyle – a lively idea, but Sullivan preferred to set *Haddon Hall* by Sydney Grundy in a style midway between the gay *Gondoliers* and the grand *Ivanhoe*. Much of it was composed at Monte Carlo during morphia-aided intermissions from the excruciating 'quarry', as he called the stones in his 'kidney'. For three months early in 1892 he was racked between his work and his sick-bed, his general condition deteriorating until he despaired of life, at forty-nine years of age. D'Oyly Carte rushed out from England. The Prince of Wales sent his surgeon, who reported that an operation on a man in such weak condition would be fatal. The operation as practised at that date was severe; the only treatment they gave Sullivan was morphia. From his agony he recovered sufficiently to return to England, a thin and haggard man. He convalesced at Sandringham with the Prince and Princess of Wales. Then he completed *Haddon Hall* and conducted the first performance at the Savoy. He rejoiced that Gilbert called at his dressing-room afterwards. During their estrangement Gilbert had got Alfred Cellier, of *Dorothy* fame, to write the music for *The Mountebanks*, a version of the Lozenge which Sullivan had spurned. W.S.G. produced it at the Globe and it had a good run, but nothing that either Gilbert or Sullivan wrote without the other has lived.

Mr and Mrs Gilbert were now living at Grim's Dyke, a Victorian pseudo-Tudor mansion amid the rhododendrons of Harrow Weald, with 110 acres of farmland, several tennis-courts, and greenhouses luscious with peaches, grapes and melons. The era's most prosperous dramatist employed forty servants in house and gardens. *Kitty's Cookery Book* prescribed for dinner-parties of up to twenty-four persons. The Gilberts had recently adopted as their daughter Nancy McIntosh, a lovely young American singer; their community also included various cats, dogs, monkeys, tame deer, doves, and a donkey named Adelina Patti after the most celebrated singer of the time. All pheasants and foxes had sanctuary in Gilbert's grounds for he abhorred blood sports: 'Deer-stalking would be a very fine sport if only the deer had guns.' His diary at this period was often written in French to foil the eyes of servants, though it records the mildest of pleasures such as his passion for bathing in his lake, and his exploits at 'croquet avec Nancy'.

Grim's Dyke was the acme of late Victorian elegance whenever a summer garden-party was held, with a band playing on the sunken lawn and horse-carriages arriving with a star cast of bishops, judges, statesmen, writers, actors and actresses (but never royalty – Gilbert wasn't Sullivan). W.S.G. was expected to scatter quips among the teacups. Once a guest told of a first night when a famous actor was for a wonder in tune, and Gilbert barked: 'Oh, I know that first-night nervousness, it soon wears off.'

Here at Grim's Dyke the plot of *Utopia Limited* was written on thirty-seven pages of a school exercise book, and the subject of its satire was Gilbert's own Victorian world. A glamorous South Sea island, peopled by the lazy subjects of King Paramount, is exposed to reform when the Princess Zara (played at the Savoy by Nancy McIntosh) returns from an emancipated English education at Girton, and strives to anglicize everything, holding England up as a Utopian model. This situation offered many targets for Gilbertian arrows: British business methods, the parliamentary system, the Law, stage censorship, the armed services, even the statuesque ladies drinking tea at Grim's Dyke: 'English girls of well-bred notions Shun all unrehearsed emotions.'

The exercise book was popped into Sullivan's bag as he left once more for the Riviera, after being entertained during his convalescence at Windsor Castle and at Grim's Dyke. A cordial note was struck in the winter of 1892–93 when Sullivan rented a villa at Cappe-Roquebrune and Gilbert travelled there to confer with him about the plot of *Utopia Limited*. 'This is a pleasant house standing in an orange garden close to the sea,' wrote Gilbert to Dearest Kits. 'A.S. extremely pleasant and hospitable.' Gilbert sped back quickly to Kitten and to his desk. Sullivan basked in the Mediterranean sun, returning to London in the spring for the opening by Queen Victoria of the Imperial Institute, South Kensington – its purpose to promote the resources of the Empire by technological research and publicity. Sir Arthur Sullivan, in levee dress, conducted before the Queen an orchestra of ninety-eight players in his own *Imperial March*; its composition had taken him three days. Then back to the score of *Utopia Limited* and its Gilbertian view of an island glorious in 'her present pre-eminent position among civilised nations'. The Anglo-Utopian idea was hard going for both Gilbert and Sullivan. They laboured slowly, leaning over backwards to meet one another's many objections. 'I will come on Thursday as you suggest,' wrote Gilbert. 'I assume that you are not averse to standing a bit of bread and cheese and a drop of beer to a pore working man wots bin out of work for some years?'

During rehearsals at the Savoy in the autumn of 1893 Gilbert's gout had him on crutches. Four years had passed since the last new Gilbert and Sullivan opera. People queued at the doors on the morning of the first performance of *Utopia Limited*, and its tumultuous reception that night proved in what estimation author and composer were still held. The most moving scene of the evening came after the cast had taken their bows: from opposite sides of the stage hobbled Gilbert, disdaining his crutches, and Sullivan, once

Nancy McIntosh, the American singer and actress whom the Gilberts adopted as their daughter.

Grim's Dyke, the Gilberts' final home, seen from the croquet
lawn. (*Left*) Paul, one of Gilbert's pet lemurs, photographed
by the dramatist himself: Paul's speciality was to sit on his
master's shoulders while he dressed for dinner, managing, 'by a
peculiar trick of shifting his hands and feet, to remain standing
as the clothes were assumed or discarded.'

Gilbert reading his new play *Utopia Limited* to the cast at the Savoy; behind him is his wife and also on the platform are Sullivan and the Cartes. Nancy McIntosh is fifth from right in the front row of stalls.

so debonair, now so frail. They stood there smiling into the auditorium which had seen so many of their triumphs, then they turned and shook hands.

Some critics thought *Utopia Limited* a resurrection pie, but Bernard Shaw gave the new Savoy opera a pat on the back in the *Saturday Review*, especially for its music. One scene was a sure-fire parody on 10 Downing Street procedure: to practise English methods King Paramount's Cabinet Ministers were ranged on chairs across the stage in the manner familiarized by Victorian audiences by the Christy Minstrels at St James's Hall, Piccadilly. With banjo, guitar, fiddles, tambourines and bones the Cabinet sang their 'nigger minstrel' skit. It was just the kind of high-spirited lark that Sullivan and Gilbert, together, could carry off with tremendous verve. It is one of those plums of Victoriana with which the Savoy Operas are stuffed. But one speech as originally given in *Utopia Limited* might (some of it) be delivered today by a critic of the deviousness of modern politicians, Princess Zara's tongue-in-cheek testimonial to English party politics: 'Government by Party! Introduce that great and glorious element – at once the bulwark and

foundation of England's greatness – and all will be well! No political measures will endure because one Party will assuredly undo all that the other Party has done; *inexperienced civilians will govern your Army and your Navy; no social reforms will be attempted because out of vice, squalor and drunkenness no political capital is to be made;* and while grouse is to be shot, and foxes worried to death, the legislative action of the country will be at a standstill.' This was attacked by the *Daily Graphic* as 'the bitterest speech Mr Gilbert has ever penned', and a small storm blew up about the words in italics above, whereupon Gilbert ordered them to be cut. This self-censorship is revealing of Gilbert himself. He was not a political rebel like Bernard Shaw, he simply loved to play the gay Guy Fawkes, blowing up politicians with abandon. During his early life he had shown signs of Liberalism, but we have seen apropos of *Iolanthe* that he may have been moving to the right. Now, in 1893, his reforming spirit was plainly not strong enough to make him stand like a Shavian crusader blowing up Parliament every night and be damned to the box office. His satirical view of the Peers' supremacy seems to have dimmed

(*Above*) 'Friends Again', a cartoon celebrating the reconciliation of Sullivan and Gilbert after the first performance of the new opera. (*Below*) Contemporary drawing of the Cabinet lined up *à la* Christy Minstrels: 'You are not making fun of us?', asks the King (in the centre). 'This is in accordance with the practice at the Court of St James's?'

The 'disgusting' Maud Allen
as Salome.

since *Iolanthe*, for 1893 would have offered the earlier Gilbert a field day: a Conservative-dominated House of Lords vetoed a Liberal government's measure for Irish home rule, crabbed English local government reform and killed an Employers' Liability Bill, so that in 1894 Prime Minister Gladstone warned the Peers that their intransigence was intolerable, and resigned. Gilbert seems to have been out of touch with Gladstone's radicalism.

In the dawn of the twentieth century he certainly swung to the right; we see the squire of Grim's Dyke as a local (and very active) magistrate, and later as Deputy-Lieutenant of Middlesex, a stout figure of the Establishment who gave liberally and privately to charities. But when Lloyd George enacted his social measures in 1908–11 W.S.G. came out strongly against nationalized welfare. In entertainment, too, he found the new century disturbing. Several of its plays are described in his diary as 'banal' or 'rot' and some as plain immoral. At the Palace (formerly Carte's Opera House) he thought the dancer Maud Allen 'disgusting'. He ridiculed the Lord Chamberlain for banning *The Mikado* during a Japanese prince's visit to England in 1907, but two years later when W.S.G. gave evidence to a parliamentary enquiry he argued for the retention of censorship: 'I think that the stage of a theatre is not a proper pulpit from which to disseminate doctrines possibly of anarchism, socialism and agnosticism. It is not the proper platform upon which to discuss questions of adultery and free love before a mixed audience composed of people of all ages, of both sexes, of all ways of thinking, of all conditions of life, and of various degrees of education.'

Gilbert drew a sharp line between what was fit in public and what was merely frivolous in private; there are many stories of his Rabelaisian tongue when outside the theatre. On the stage he made clean fun pay. His principles were based on firm Victorian ideas of what was proper for the good of society, but this basic rule did not deprive the operas of wit. On the contrary, Gilbert's stage career proved that in light entertainment the early Victorian slapstick burlesques and stage pornography could be replaced by comic operas of both high quality and wide popularity.

Utopia Limited's lack of staying power is peculiar. After a good original run of 245 performances in 1893–94 it has never been revived in London. The reason is that in their anxiety to return with a bang the Savoy Trinity put on an over-ambitious opera, making unusually exacting demands on the cast and entailing lavish staging, and therefore high cost. It was the most expensive production of all the operas, costing £7,200. Moreover, compared with *The Gondoliers*, it betrayed a fading humour. Since the Carpet Quarrel relationships had not been easy, despite a show of comradeship. Now there was no great urge to collaborate. Sullivan and Gilbert began to think of themselves as declining in physique, each in his own characteristic way.

Gilbert, aged fifty-eight, wrote in 1894: 'I am a crumbling man – a magnificent ruin, no doubt, but still a ruin – and like all ruins I look best by moonlight. Give me a sprig of ivy and an owl under my arm and Tintern Abbey would not be in it with me.' In fact, apart from gout, his health was robust. Sullivan, fifty-two in that year, a £20,000-a-year man, was racing his own horses, gambling extensively, taking things easily and expensively. Failing health curbed his work. He found rare satisfaction in his music for

The erstwhile iconoclast of the *Bab Ballads* proudly displaying his uniform as Deputy-Lieutenant of Middlesex and (*below*) at home at Grim's Dyke.

Sir Arthur Sullivan: 'Health is the secret of happiness', he lamented wistfully in his diary.

Comyns Carr's play *King Arthur*, produced in 1895 by Henry Irving at the Lyceum with Ellen Terry as Guinevere: the subject had a peculiar nostalgia for Sullivan, for had not Rachel Scott Russell urged him to write an Arthurian grand opera thirty years ago? After the Irving production he contemplated using some of its music later in the long-discussed opera. He never wrote it.

Richard D'Oyly Carte had grown older but not wiser; he still believed 'G and S' to be the magic box-office formula for the Savoy, and at last got the old partners together again. Their fourteenth and last comic opera, *The Grand Duke*, had the usual brilliant first night in 1896, but Gilbert said of it: 'I'm not at all a proud Mother, and I never want to see the ugly misshapen little brat again!' Sullivan fled to Monte Carlo and wrote to an old friend: 'I arrived here dead beat and feel better already. Another week's rehearsal with W.S.G. and I should have gone raving mad. I had already ordered some straw for my hair.' He wandered on to Lucerne, seeking relaxation and finding an autumnal romance with an English girl from an élite musical family. He proposed marriage. But at twenty years of age 'Miss Violet' could not see herself as Lady Sullivan.

The Grand Duke collapsed at 123 performances, the shortest run of any Gilbert and Sullivan opera since *Thespis*, twenty-five years before. Carte immediately brought back *The Mikado*, the box office was besieged, and this wonderful winner raced on to its one thousandth London performance.

The first of a series of notes from Sullivan to 'Miss Violet', the object of his last affections. The final note was written after she had rejected his marriage proposal on the day the composer called 'the most miserable I have ever spent'.

A gala evening was therefore held on 31 October 1896 (actually the 1,037th performance), with Sullivan and Gilbert taking their traditional bows. Carte was absent ill, but the gentle hand of Helen was seen in the theatre's adornment in bunting of Japanese silk, in the famed electric lights concealed within huge Japanese lanterns and in the chrysanthemums which festooned the auditorium.

During the last three years of Sullivan's life, in sudden bursts of energy between spells of sickness, he composed three light operas without Gilbert. The fade-out was tragic. At a special revival of *The Sorcerer* on its twenty-first anniversary in 1898 Sullivan and Gilbert bowed to the Savoy audience but uttered not a word to each other. It was the last time they met. But a tremendous boost to Sullivan's spirits came at that year's Leeds Musical Festival when his popularity after eighteen years of work there was marked by ovations such as even he had never experienced: 'The chorus cheered me so tremendously that I suddenly broke down, and ran off the orchestra crying like a child. When I came out of my room again, all the chorus was waiting for me, and I shook hands with them all.'

The rising young composer Edward Elgar was present that year to conduct the first performance of his *Caractacus*. He wrote to Sullivan: 'I could not let the last night of rehearsals go by without sending my thanks to you for making my "chance" possible. This is, of course, only what one knows you would do but it contrasts very much with what some people do to a person unconnected with the Schools, friendless and alone.' At this period Elgar was composing the *Enigma Variations*, musical pictures of the composer's friends; he sketched an orchestral portrait of Sullivan but eventually dropped it because its style seemed incompatible with the other *Variations*. An admirer of Sullivan's *Golden Legend*, Elgar defended him stoutly in later years. Today there is an assumption that Sullivan's oratorio was smothered in ecclesiastical overtones derived from his early musical training but Dr Percy Young writes (1971) that in the general context of Victorian choral music it 'represented a departure from the overriding convention of religiosity, and by so doing helped to emancipate music from the shackles by which it was bound. There is no doubt that Elgar, in particular, was influenced by Sullivan's boldness of conception. . . .' One must place this re-assessment alongside Sullivan's genius in comic opera to appreciate what a remarkable composer he was.

One of his best-selling popular songs, 'The Absent-minded Beggar', came with the South African war in 1899. The conjunction of music by Sullivan and words by Kipling, produced against a background of troops sailing to fight the Boers while the British public indulged in a militant orgy, might be expected to beat all records for chauvinism; actually this was a protest song against a dreadful social system which sent soldiers to war so badly paid, and coming from such poverty-stricken homes, that a charity was organized by the *Daily Mail* to raise £100,000 for the families left behind. It was called the 'Absent-minded Beggar Fund', after the song, which had a tune 'guaranteed to pull teeth out of barrel-organs', said Kipling.

In 1900 on a pathetic quest for health Sullivan wandered from spa to spa on the Continent, writing to Helen Carte: 'Physical pain and nervous terror combined are not conducive to good mental work.' Back in London

Tunbridge Wells.

Weather changed. Very cold – damp & dull. Cellier & I indoors all day (except for half an hour's stroll) working at accomp^t to new opera.

note to Princess Christian, & Clot: to say I was coming home tomorrow.

Have been here just a fortnight, and what have I done? little more than nothing, first from illness and physical incapability, secondly from <u>brooding</u>, and nervous terror about myself. D^r hanser examined me very carefully this morning – chest. heart, lungs &c – says I am sound enough, but my throat still in a bad state. But practically I have done nothing for a month. Have **15 MONDAY [288–77]** now finished & framed **Quarter Sessions Week.** (9h 51m 1st Act, & they are rehearsing it. **A.M. (Greenwich)**

<u>Lovely day.</u> Fr: Cellier left at 11.10. I am sorry to leave such a lovely day.

on an unusually bright mid-October day he wrote the last words in his diary: 'I am sorry to leave such a lovely day.' Brighter, too, was the atmosphere between the Savoy Trinity, thanks to Helen Carte. Supervising a coming revival of _Patience_ she suggested a public reconciliation in which the three partners should take bows together – or, she suggested lightly, what about a procession of bath-chairs along the footlights? The three responded cordially, but on the first night Sullivan was too sick to join the others. 'Pray tell Gilbert how very much I feel the disappointment. Good luck to you all. Three invalid chairs would have looked very well from the front.'

Gilbert to Sullivan: 'The old opera woke up splendidly.' Clay-puddling his lake at Grim's Dyke, he had caught rheumatic fever and was ordered on a health cruise to Egypt. 'I sincerely hope to find you all right again on my return,' says his last letter to 'My dear Sullivan'. Ten days later, in the small hours of 22 November 1900, Arthur Sullivan died of bronchitis at the age of fifty-eight. Only his nephew Herbert, his valet and his housekeeper were present. Mrs Ronalds rushed in a cab to Queen's Mansions, to find all the blinds drawn.

The Queen ordered a State funeral, the first part held at the Chapel Royal, the second at St Paul's Cathedral. The cortège passed the Savoy on its way along the Thames Embankment, the band of the Scots Guards playing the Dead March from _Saul_. Just across the river was Lambeth and the tiny

(_Left_) The final entries in Sullivan's diary and (_right_) the last photograph of the composer, haggard, ill and close to death.

Sullivan's funeral in St Paul's Cathedral. François Cellier and Sir John Stainer, composer of *The Crucifixion*, are among the pall-bearers.

terrace-house where Sullivan had first practised at the parlour piano. Sir Arthur now lies in the crypt at St Paul's.

Within a few months Richard D'Oyly Carte too was dead. The old century had slipped away, and the old Queen with it. The Victorian age was ended, and there was a curious finality about it. William Morris, Lewis Carroll, Gladstone, Ruskin, du Maurier, Wilde, Sullivan – they all died in the last few years of the Victorian century. The infant voices of George Gershwin and Noel Coward joined the snort of the motor-car to herald a faster and noisier century. W. S. Gilbert, who from the turn of the century lived on for another decade, growing ever younger in a properly Gilbertian fashion, bought one of the first horseless carriages in the district, an American Locomobile steam-car: 'I made my début by spoiling a parson.' This was the first of a number of horseless carriages on which he adventured 'avec Mrs. et Nancy', says the diary. 'Le motor tres bien sur le top speed, beaucoup de bruit au middle speed.' His new interests included astronomy, country walks, visits to the cinematograph ('tres bien') and spells of developing ('photo-graphie – pas de success'). Helen D'Oyly Carte's revivals of his operas gave him the opportunity to pop into the Savoy with new bonhomie and some-times old-fashioned irascibility. He updated *The Mikado* a little to suit twentieth-century politics, adding to the Lord High Executioner's little list such persons as 'The lovely suffragist – I've got her on the list' and 'The red-hot Socialist – I don't think he'll be missed'. His tardy knighthood in 1907, twenty-four years after Sullivan's, gave him the opportunity to flay the curious system of honours which so often puts writers behind musicians and actors in the queue for 'a tin-pot two-penny-halfpenny sort of distinction'.

On a lovely May afternoon in 1911 Sir William Gilbert, full of vigour at seventy-four years of age, took two young women bathing in his lake. One got out of her depth and began to struggle. Sir William dived in to her aid. The two women survived, but when they pulled Gilbert out he was dead from the sudden exertion. He lies without ostentation in the parish churchyard at Stanmore, not far from Grim's Dyke. Gilbert left £111,971; Sullivan £54,527. In death they were as different as in life, but these fortunes matter little – the true richness is that these men made a revolution in the whole field of entertainment.

Many things that they themselves thought eternal have been thrown into the dustcart with the discarded monarchies, the rejected moral codes, the exploded scientific, religious and social beliefs, the hansom cabs and bustles and whatnots of Victoriana, and yet through this cataclysm a few wildly nonsensical and occasionally sentimental comic operas have persisted, and

The lake at Grim's Dyke, photographed by W.S.G.; in it he met his death.

Commemorative plaques of Sullivan (from St Paul's Cathedral) and Gilbert (from the Embankment in London).

will persist. Sub-standard performances have done some damage to the reputation of Gilbert and Sullivan operas but in the final analysis they stand on two rocks as classics: firstly, their nonsense and their sentiment express something basic in the Anglo-Saxon character – 'I know of no more English artistic expression,' says Sir Adrian Boult; and secondly, the sheer professionalism of their creators gives a quality that endures. Igor Stravinsky, interviewed in the *New York Times* in 1968, recalled that he had been introduced to the operas by Serge Diaghilev, who had enjoyed translating the songs into Russian for his own amusement. Stravinsky went on to compare Gilbert and Sullivan to the collaboration of Strauss and Hofmannsthal: 'The British team is never boring. The operas gallop along like happy colts, not like cart horses. They are also moral. The characters are good and bad, and the moral is always clearly drawn, although I do not overlook the sophistication of the satire. They remind me of American Western films or plays when these are of top-notch quality. While they depend on conventions, their attack on conventions is always progressive. This is undoubtedly one of the major reasons for the continued popularity of the operas.'

ACKNOWLEDGMENTS

For their advice and for access to documents the author wishes to thank the Queen's Librarian, Windsor Castle (Mr Robert Mackworth-Young); Miss Bridget D'Oyly Carte and her staff; Dr Percy M. Young; Mr Reginald Allen, whose Gilbert and Sullivan collection is at the Pierpont Morgan Library, New York; Mr Brian Rust; the British Post Office Records; Mr Alan Wykes, of the Savage Club; Mr J. F. R. Withycombe, of Cambridge; Dr R. B. Chalmers of Saffron Walden; and Mr Colin Prestige, editor of *The Gilbert and Sullivan Journal* (London), whose lecture to an international conference at Kansas University in 1970 threw new light on American productions, especially those piratical.

Librarians have as usual shown helpfulness and efficiency, especially those of: the British Museum, Cambridge University, the City of Leeds (Mr A. B. Craven), the Royal Academy of Music, the Saffron Walden reference library, the London Library, the Enthoven Collection (Victoria and Albert Museum), the Royal Colleges of Surgeons and of Physicians, and King's College, London University.

The following persons, closely associated with the principals in this story but now deceased, gave me original material for *The Gilbert and Sullivan Book*, some of which is incorporated in the present volume: Mr Rupert D'Oyly Carte, Miss Nancy McIntosh, Mrs Elena Bashford, Mrs Mary Carter (niece of Sir William Gilbert), and Mrs Elgar-Blake (daughter of Sir Edward Elgar).

Sir Lindsay Wellington as Controller of the BBC Home Service decided in 1947 to chance his arm (and mine) in planning a six-part radio biography on *The Lives of Gilbert and Sullivan*, a series on a scale unprecedented in those days. These programmes (since repeated many times) led me to a film of which I was co-writer with Mr Sidney Gilliat, and to my two books on this subject. So to Sir Lindsay, godfather of the original idea, and to other old colleagues at the BBC, I express here my gratitude for stimulating my efforts at research in so delightful a direction.

Nor can I omit my thanks to the staff of Thames and Hudson Ltd for their collaboration in the production of the present book.

BIBLIOGRAPHY

From the large number of publications on the subject of Gilbert and Sullivan the following may be recommended:

Allen, Reginald, *The First Night Gilbert and Sullivan*, New York, 1958
Goldberg, Isaac, *The Story of Gilbert and Sullivan*, London, 1929
Jacobs, Arthur, *Gilbert and Sullivan*, London, 1957
Lawrence, Arthur, *Sir Arthur Sullivan*, London, 1899
Pearson, Hesketh, *Gilbert, His Life and Strife*, London, 1957
Rollins, Cyril, and Witts, R. John, *The D'Oyly Carte Company in Gilbert and Sullivan Operas*, London, 1962
Sullivan, Herbert, and Flower, Newman, *Sir Arthur Sullivan*, London, 1927
Williamson, Audrey, *Gilbert and Sullivan Opera*, London, 1955
Young, Percy M., *Sir Arthur Sullivan*, London, 1971
The Gilbert and Sullivan Journal

ON ALLIED SUBJECTS

Baldwin, F. G. C., *The History of the Telephone in the United Kingdom*, London, 1925
Chesterton, G. K., essay in de la Mare, Walter, ed., *The Eighteen-Eighties*, Cambridge, 1930
Graves, Charles L., *The Life and Letters of Sir George Grove*, London, 1903
Grove, George, appendix to Kreissle von Hellborn, Heinrich, *The Life of Franz Schubert*, tr. Coleridge, 2 vols, London, 1869
Macgeorge, Ethel, *The Life and Reminiscences of Jessie Bond*, London, 1930
Pennell, E. R. and J., *The Life of James McNeill Whistler*, 2 vols, London, 1908
Rogers, Clara, *Memories of a Musical Career*, Boston, 1919
Scholes, Percy, *The Mirror of Music*, 2 vols, London, 1947
Spark, Fred R., and Bennett, Joseph, *History of the Leeds Musical Festival*, Leeds, 1892

CHRONOLOGY

1836 18 November: W.S. Gilbert born, Strand.

1842 13 May: Arthur Sullivan born, Lambeth.

1844 Richard D'Oyly Carte born, Soho.

1845 Tom Sullivan appointed bandmaster at the Royal Military College, Sandhurst. The Sullivans move to Camberley.

1854 Sullivan admitted to the Chapel Royal.

1855 Sullivan's first published composition: 'O Israel'.

1856 Sullivan wins Mendelssohn Scholarship to the Royal Academy of Music.

1857 Gilbert takes a degree at King's College and becomes a clerk in the Civil Service.

1858 Sullivan wins scholarship to the Leipzig Conservatory.

1861 Gilbert called to the Bar; starts to write the *Bab Ballads*. Sullivan's *The Tempest* performed, Leipzig.

1862 5 April: *The Tempest*, Crystal Palace.

1864 14 May: Sullivan's ballet, *L'Ile Enchantée*, Covent Garden. 8 September: Sullivan's masque, *Kenilworth*, Birmingham Festival.

1866 10 March: Sullivan's symphony, *In Ireland*, Crystal Palace. Death of Tom Sullivan. 30 October: Sullivan's *In Memoriam*, Norwich Festival. 24 November: Sullivan's cello concerto, Crystal Palace. Gilbert's burlesque *Dulcamara*, St James's Theatre.

1867 6 August: Gilbert marries Lucy Agnes Turner, St Mary Abbot's, Kensington. Gilbert's pantomime, *Harlequin Cock-Robin*, Lyceum. Sullivan and Burnand write *Cox and Box*, *The Contrabandista*. Sullivan and Grove discover lost Schubert manuscripts in Vienna.

1868 21 December: Gilbert's 'operatic extravaganza', *Robert le Diable*, Gaiety Theatre.

1869 Sullivan appointed professor at the Royal Academy of Music. Sullivan meets Gilbert at the Royal Gallery of Illustration. 8 September: Sullivan's oratorio, *The Prodigal Son*, Worcester Cathedral. Gilbert's *Bab Ballads* first published as a book.

1870 Gilbert's play, *The Princess*. Sullivan's *Overture di Ballo*, Norwich Festival.

1871 Tennyson-Sullivan song cycle, *The Window, or the Loves of the Wrens*. Gilbert's play *Pygmalion and Galatea*, Haymarket Theatre.

26 December: first Gilbert-Sullivan opera, *Thespis*.

1872 Rachel Scott Russell and Sullivan break off engagement. Sullivan's hymn, 'Onward Christian Soldiers', and his *Te Deum* for the recovery of the Prince of Wales.

1873 27 August: Sullivan's oratorio, *The Light of the World*, Birmingham Festival.

1874 Gilbert's plays *Charity* and *Sweethearts*, Haymarket Theatre. Sullivan appointed editor of the SPCK Hymnal; writes the music for *The Merry Wives of Windsor*, Gaiety Theatre.

1875 25 March: *Trial by Jury*, Royalty Theatre. 15 November: *Trial by Jury* (pirate production), Eagle Theatre, New York. 9 December: Gilbert's play *Broken Hearts*, Court Theatre. Sullivan appointed conductor of the Glasgow Orpheus Choir (until 1877).

1876 Sullivan appointed principal of the National Training School of Music (until 1881). Sullivan receives honorary doctorate of music, Cambridge University. Comedy Opera Company founded.

1877 17 November: *The Sorcerer*, Opéra Comique.

Death of Fred Sullivan; Arthur writes 'The Lost Chord'.
Mrs Ronalds assumes the role of Sullivan's confidante from about this year onwards.

1878 25 May: *H.M.S. Pinafore*, Opéra Comique.

1879 Sullivan receives honorary degree, Oxford University.
Dispute with Comedy Opera Company; partnership formed between Gilbert, Sullivan and Carte.
First amateur G. & S. performance licensed in Britain, Kingston-on-Thames.
Many pirate productions of *H.M.S. Pinafore* in America.
1 December: *H.M.S. Pinafore* (Carte production), Fifth Avenue Theatre, New York.
30 December: British première of *The Pirates of Penzance*, Paignton.
31 December: U.S. première (Carte production), Fifth Avenue Theatre, New York.

1880 3 April: *The Pirates of Penzance*, Opéra Comique.
October: Sullivan's first Leeds Musical Festival; his sacred cantata, *The Martyr of Antioch*, words adapted by Gilbert.

1881 23 April: *Patience*, Opéra Comique.
22 September: *Patience* (Carte production), Standard Theatre, New York.
10 October: opening of the Savoy Theatre with *Patience* and the introduction of electric lighting to the theatre.
Sullivan visits the monarchs of Europe with the Duke of Edinburgh.
Sullivan moves to Queen's Mansions, Victoria Street.

1882 25 November: *Iolanthe*, Savoy Theatre and Standard Theatre, New York.

1883 22 May: Sullivan knighted.
Gilberts move to Harrington Gardens, Kensington.
Historic experiment with broadcasting, Leeds.

1884 5 January: *Princess Ida*, Savoy Theatre.
11 February: *Princess Ida* (Carte production), Fifth Avenue Theatre, New York.
Sullivan's first decision to write no more comic opera; row with Gilbert.

1885 14 March: *The Mikado*, Savoy Theatre.
19 August: *The Mikado* (Carte production), Fifth Avenue Theatre, New York.
Pirate productions innumerable of *The Mikado*, New York.

1886 16 October: Sullivan's oratorio, *The Golden Legend*, Leeds.
Several Carte companies tour U.S.A. and Canada.

1887 22 January: *Ruddigore*, Savoy Theatre.
21 February: *Ruddigore* (Carte production), Fifth Avenue Theatre, New York.
22 June: Queen Victoria's Diamond Jubilee; Sullivan's 'Jubilee Ode'.

1888 3 October: *The Yeomen of the Guard*, Savoy Theatre.
17 October: *The Yeomen of the Guard* (Carte production), Casino Theatre, New York.

1889 D'Oyly Carte opens the Savoy Hotel. Gilbert and Sullivan quar-

rel about the relative weight of their contributions to the operas.
7 December: *The Gondoliers*, Savoy Theatre.

1890 7 January: *The Gondoliers* (Carte production), Park Theatre, New York.
The Carpet Quarrel.
Gilbert buys Grim's Dyke, Harrow Weald.

1891 31 January: Carte's English Opera House opened with Sullivan's *Ivanhoe*.

1892 Sullivan falls seriously ill at Monte Carlo.

1893 7 October: *Utopia Limited*, Savoy Theatre.
Sullivan's *Imperial March* for the opening of the Imperial Institute.

1894 26 March: *Utopia Limited* (Carte production), Broadway Theatre, New York.

1895 Sullivan's incidental music to *King Arthur*.

1896 7 March: the last Gilbert and Sullivan opera, *The Grand Duke*, Savoy Theatre.

1898 Sullivan's last Leeds Festival.

1899 Kipling-Sullivan song: 'The Absent-minded Beggar'.

1900 22 November: death of Sullivan.

1901 3 April: death of D'Oyly Carte.

1907 *The Mikado* banned during the visit of a Japanese prince to England.
15 July: Gilbert knighted.

1911 29 May: death of Gilbert.

LIST OF ILLUSTRATIONS

62 Poster for the première of *The Pirates of Penzance*, Royal Bijou Theatre, Paignton, December 1879. Photo the author's collection

Programme cover for *The Pirates of Penzance*, Opéra Comique, 1880. Victoria and Albert Museum, London

63 Marion Hood as Mabel in *The Pirates of Penzance*, Opéra Comique, 1880. Photo the author's collection

64 Broadway, New York, 1882. Mansell Collection

65 Page from Sullivan's diary showing his net receipts from 1 January to 31 December 1881. Photo the author's collection

66 Sullivan conducting; engraving from *Punch*, 30 October 1880

68 Embroidered panels for the Red House by William Morris, *c.* 1860. Victoria and Albert Museum, London

The three soldiers as aesthetes from *Patience*, Opéra Comique, 1881. Victoria and Albert Museum. London. Photo Mrs Grygierczyk

69 'An aesthetic midday meal'; engraving by George du Maurier from *Punch*, 17 July 1880

Scene from Sadler's Wells Opera's production of *Patience*, London Coliseum, 1972. Sadler's Wells Press Office. Photo Donald Southern

70 'Rossetti's name is heard in America'; watercolour by Max Beerbohm, 1916. Tate Gallery, London

72 Interior of the Savoy Theatre during a performance of *Patience*; engraving from the *Graphic*, 17 December 1881. Mansell Collection

73 Programme for *Patience*, Savoy Theatre, 1881. British Museum, London

74 Queen's Mansions, London. Photo by courtesy of the Gilbert and Sullivan Society

75 Interior of Sullivan's flat, Queen's Mansions, London; photograph from Arthur J. Wells's *Souvenir of Sir Arthur Sullivan*, 1901

76 Pen drawings by Gilbert from his plot-book for *Iolanthe*, 1882. Photo the author's collection

77 Scenes from *Iolanthe*, Savoy Theatre; engraving from the *Graphic*, 23 December 1882. Victoria and Albert Museum, London

78 Harrington Gardens, London. Photo the author

79 Library at Harrington Gardens, London; photo from one of Gilbert's albums. British Museum, London, MSS Add. 49353A, f. 6

Richard Wagner

81 Opera at home; engraving from the *Strand Magazine*, September 1898. Westminster Public Libraries

82 Scene from *Princess Ida*, Savoy Theatre; engraving from the *Illustrated London News*, 19 January 1884. Mansell Collection

83 'An advertising Carte'; engraving from *Punch*, 9 December 1882

84 Japanese girls; photograph from one of Gilbert's albums. British Museum, London, MSS Add. 49352, f. 13

Sybil Grey, Leonora Braham and Jessie Bond as the Three Little Maids in *The Mikado*, Savoy Theatre, 1885. Photo the author's collection

Advertisement for Liberty and Co. from the programme for *The Mikado*, Savoy Theatre, 1885. Victoria and Albert Museum, London

85 Scene from a recent production of *The Mikado* by the D'Oyly Carte Opera Company. Bridget D'Oyly Carte Ltd

Costume designs for *The Mikado*; watercolours by Charles Ricketts, 1926. Victoria and Albert Museum, London

86 Poster for the *Swing Mikado*, Civic Opera House, Chicago, 1947. Photo the author's collection

87 Self-caricature by Gilbert; pen drawing for Helen M'Ilworth. Trustees of the Pierpont Morgan Library, New York

88 'The Ironmaster at the Savoy'; engraving, 1881. Victoria and Albert Museum, London

89 Reception for Franz Liszt in London; engraving from the *Graphic*, 17 April 1886. Victoria and Albert Museum, London

Leeds Musical Festival; engraving from the *Illustrated London News*, 23 October 1886. Victoria and Albert Museum, London

90 Cartoon on the title *Ruddygore*; engraving from the *Illustrated Sporting and Dramatic News*, 5 February 1887

Richard Temple as Sir Roderick Murgatroyd in *Ruddigore*, Savoy

Theatre; engraving, from the *Illustrated Sporting and Dramatic News*, 1887

91 Jubilee Procession, 1897. British Museum, London

92 Beefeater; pen drawing by Gilbert, *c*. 1888. Photo the author's collection

93 Rhoda Maitland as Elsie and Henry Lytton as Jack Point in *The Yeomen of the Guard*, 1888. Photo the author's collection

Richard Temple as Meryll in *The Yeomen of the Guard*, Savoy Theatre, 1888. Photo the author's collection

94 Monte Carlo Casino; engraving by Jean Bèraud, 1890. Mansell Collection

95 Savoy scaffolding, 1888; etching by James Abbott McNeill Whistler. Bridget D'Oyly Carte Ltd

James Abbott McNeill Whistler; painting by Walter Greaves. National Portrait Gallery, London

96 Savoy Hotel, 1889. Photo National Monuments Record

Royal English Opera House, London; lithograph from the *Graphic*, 31 January 1891. Mansell Collection

97 Richard D'Oyly Carte; caricature by 'Spy' from *Vanity Fair*, 14 February 1891. The Raymond Mander and Joe Mitchenson Theatre Collection

98 Pages from Gilbert's plot-book for *The Gondoliers*, 1889. British Museum, London, MSS Add. 49313, ff. 62v–63

99 Scene from *The Gondoliers*, Savoy

Theatre; engraving from the *Illustrated London News*, December 1889. Mansell Collection

Page of Sullivan's score for *The Gondoliers*, 1889. British Museum, London, MSS Add. 53779, f. 103v

100 'Once upon a time there were two kings'; engraving from *Punch*, 4 January 1890

103 Scene from *Ivanhoe*, Royal English Opera House; engraving from the *Illustrated London News*, 31 January 1891. Victoria and Albert Museum, London

104 Performance of *The Gondoliers* before Queen Victoria at Windsor Castle; engraving from the *Illustrated London News*, 31 January 1891. Victoria and Albert Museum, London

106 Nancy McIntosh, 1895. Victoria and Albert Museum, London. Photo Mrs Grygierczyk

107 Grim's Dyke, Harrow; photograph from one of Gilbert's albums. British Museum, London, MSS Add. 49353D, f. 8v

Gilbert's pet lemur; photograph by Gilbert. Trustees of the Pierpont Morgan Library, New York

108 Gilbert reading *Utopia Limited* to the actors at the Savoy Theatre, 1893; photogravure. Mansell Collection

109 'Friends Again'; title-page of the *Pall Mall Budget*, 12 October 1893. Westminster Public Libraries

Cabinet Ministers as Nigger Minstrels in *Utopia Limited*, Savoy Theatre; engraving from *Harper's Magazine*, 1893

110 Maud Allen as Salome. Mansell Collection

111 Two soldiers; engraving by Gilbert from his *Bab Ballads*, 1870

Gilbert as Deputy-Lieutenant of Middlesex, 1891. Trustees of the Pierpont Morgan Library, New York

Gilbert at his home at Grim's Dyke, Harrow. Photo the author's collection

112 Sir Arthur Sullivan in the 1890s. Mansell Collection

113 Letter from Sullivan to 'Miss Violet', written at the Grand Hotel National, Lucerne, 1896. Photo the author's collection

115 Last entries in Sullivan's diary, 15 October 1900. Photo the author's collection

Last photograph of Sullivan, 1900

116 Funeral of Sullivan in St Paul's Cathedral; engraving from the *Graphic*, December 1900. Radio Times Hulton Picture Library

117 Grim's Dyke pond; photograph from one of Gilbert's albums. British Museum, London, MSS Add. 49353D, f. 3

118 Sullivan's memorial plaque by William Goscombe John. Crypt of St Paul's Cathedral, London. Reproduced by courtesy of the Dean and Chapter of St Paul's Cathedral

Gilbert's memorial plaque by George Frampton, 1914. Victoria Embankment, London. Radio Times Hulton Picture Library

INDEX

Page numbers in italics refer to illustrations